"What we believe about ourselves is shaped most deeply by what we believe about God, and by what He says is true of us. But often, the truth can be buried under years of lies. In *Am I Loved?*, Shawn digs down to the roots of unbelief and replaces those lies with the most powerful of all truths. Read this book to apprehend the depth of the Father's love for you!"

Caesar Kalinowski
Author of *Transformed* and *The Gospel Primer*

"The phrase in the book, '. . . a boy looks for safety and security, expecting others to create it; a man creates safety and security and invites others into it," spoke to me. I had to look in the mirror and ask, "Am I a boy or a man?" This book speaks to those deep, innermost, and often unspoken questions: *Who am I really?* and *Am I loved?* Read it and you're on your journey to knowing and believing the truth."

George Petrie
President & CEO of Goodman Real Estate

"The subject Jesus so often addressed was belief. Shawn invites us into the sanctuary of his inner life to catch a glimpse of the transforming power of believing in Jesus. Shawn shares how God reveals to each of us the incredibly beautiful creature He crafted when He made us in His image. Our lives will never be the same when we truly embrace the truth that we are loved."

Doug Burleigh
Former President of Young Life

"*Don't* read this book if you prefer dishonesty over truth, or hiding rather than standing in the light. *Do* read it if you long to live more fully in the freedom of God's love. With stunning honesty and awareness, Shawn takes us on a long journey through his own brokenness as he lets the Spirit carry him through profound insights from Scripture into the heart of the Father. His writing is an invitation to allow the 'Divine Therapist' to walk with us into our own pain and brokenness. He offers engaging practices to open our hearts to the healing love of God."

Dr. Tim Dearborn
Author of *Taste and See* and *Business as a Holy Calling*

"Shawn invites us to confront our most compelling question—*Do I matter?* His poignant honesty takes the reader on a journey to answer this question once and for all: *You are beloved of God—there is no higher value.* This is the cornerstone on which our lives and our faith, and thus our decisions, ultimately depend."

Dr. Tina Schermer Sellers
Author of *Sex, God, and the Conservative Church*

"A deeply personal story and a wisely sculpted invitation to challenge those destructive mantras that play on a loop in our heads telling us who we 'really' are. A shining light to this searching pilgrim that, beyond the dogma and the drama, maybe God's identity could simply and literally be love."

Sean McConnell, Singer/Songwriter

'Am I Loved?' is a powerful book that delves deep into God's unending love for mankind. So many people today are searching for meaning, belonging, and ultimately, love. As you read through the book you can feel God's heart yearn for a personal relationship with each of us. It's intoxicating . . . specifically during a time when mankind is searching—in all the wrong places—for that which God has already provided . . . His love."

Dustin Stoker
Chief Operations Officer,
The Northwest Seaport Alliance

"Shawn wastes no time asking one of the most deeply rooted questions of all humanity: 'Am I loved?' There is not a single person that wouldn't benefit from diving into this book and finding the answer. This kind of heart work isn't comfortable, but Shawn makes it simple. Even the most confused among us will walk away from this book having a greater sense of purpose."

Brooke Sailer
Author of *This Thing Called Home*

"Am I Loved?" gets at the universal questions of identity, worth, and faith everyone grapples with, along with practical guidance on how to answer them."

Ron Carucci, Managing Partner of Navalent,
Harvard Business Review & Forbes Contributor

Am I Loved?

The Question You Might
Not Know You're Asking

Shawn Petree

Am I Loved? The Question You Might Not Know You're Asking
First Edition, 2018

Copyright © 2018 by Shawn Petree

Scripture quotations are identified as follows:

Scripture quotations marked (AMP) are taken from the Amplified® Bible (AMP), Copyright © 2015 by The Lockman Foundation. Used by permission. www.Lockman.org.

Scripture quotations taken from the New American Standard Bible® (NASB), Copyright © 1960, 1962, 1963, 1968, 1971, 1972, 1973, 1975, 1977, 1995 by The Lockman Foundation Used by permission. www.Lockman.org

Scripture quotations marked (NIV) are taken from the Holy Bible, New International Version®, NIV®. Copyright © 1973, 1978, 1984, 2011 by Biblica, Inc.™ Used by permission of Zondervan. All rights reserved worldwide. www.zondervan.com The "NIV" and "New International Version" are trademarks registered in the United States Patent and Trademark Office by Biblica, Inc.™

Scripture quotations marked (NLT) are taken from the Holy Bible, New Living Translation, copyright ©1996, 2004, 2007, 2013, 2015 by Tyndale House Foundation. Used by permission of Tyndale House Publishers, Inc., Carol Stream, Illinois 60188. All rights reserved.

Scripture quotations marked "Phillips" are taken from The New Testament in Modern English, copyright © 1958, 1959, 1960 J.B. Phillips and 1947, 1952, 1955, 1957 The Macmillian Company, New York. Used by permission. All rights reserved.

To order additional books:
www.amazon.com
www.amiloved.org

E-book also available

ISBN: 978-0-9996824-0-1

Editorial and Book Production: Inspira Literary Solutions, Gig Harbor, WA
Cover Design: Brianna Showalter
Interior design and typesetting: PerfecType, Nashville, TN
Printed in the USA

Acknowledgments

As you will see in this book, I believe in doing life as "we" not just "me." Working on this project, and having this book become a reality, has definitely been a "we."

The first person to acknowledge is my wife, Anna. There is no way to adequately "acknowledge" who Anna is to me, and the impact that she has had on my journey of believing the truth about myself. She is my best friend and the one who has had a front row seat to the good, the bad, and the ugly the past twenty years. Specifically, Anna is the main one I chose to process everything in life with, including this book.

Next, my sister Angela Carter. She was an English and Communications teacher for twenty years, and an excellent writer. She helped me with a lot of the first and second iterations of the manuscript.

Dennis Cagwin is a "wordsmith" extraordinaire! If I showed you some of the paragraphs that I sent him years ago in the original manuscript, and then showed you his suggested re-write of the same paragraphs, you might be wondering if he is the author of this book and not me.

Arlyn Lawrence, along with the team at Inspira Literary Solutions, for their invaluable support through coaching, training, and overall editing and book production. As a first time author I didn't know what I didn't know, and they filled in the gaps and then some.

This book would literally have not become a reality without the incredible support of the couples from our marriage group. During a long dinner together one evening, I told the story of feeling compelled to write this book, the years I had spent working on the manuscript, and the response I had received from the team at Inspira about the original manuscript. Our friends asked when the book would be coming out, and Anna told them the project was on hold until we came up with the funds needed for editing, cover art, publishing, etc. Our friends responded with overwhelming generosity and said, "Let's get this book out together."

My three friends Bradd, Zack, and Brian for forming a "launch team," walking closely with me for the past year to methodically work behind the scenes on website, marketing, and logistics to get everything in order to launch a first book.

Gabe, for pushing me to dream big about this project and for spending time helping me clarify title of the book, purpose, and scope. Chad, for his important contribution. Jim and Ron who read the first manuscript and gave vital insight on how much work I really needed to do in order to turn the project into a readable book.

A special thanks to each friend who took the time to let me interview them about their own journey of learning to believe the truth about their identity, and to the many others along the way who encouraged and prayed for me. I know if I tried to list you all by name I would forget someone. Please know I am so very, very grateful for you all.

Table of Contents

Introduction

> *"The greatest thing you'll ever learn is to love and be loved."*
>
> ~ *Nat King Cole*

It was 1997—a drizzly, gray day in April—and I was sitting at my desk at the accounting firm where I worked at the time. I remember thinking to myself, "I really like working with numbers, but people fascinate me much more." At the time, I was volunteering with Young Life, a non-profit organization that builds relationships with teenagers and they had offered me an internship. Right there in that moment at my desk, I decided to leave my job, begin the internship, and attend seminary. I had deep, philosophical questions about the fundamental nature of life and the human heart, and I was thirsty for answers.

Over the next few years, I poured myself into philanthropic work and ministry. I jumped from a lonely, Type-A, hard-charging workaholic to a man learning to love others, study God's Word, and discover more about what makes us tick the way we do. It was the start of a lifelong, transformational journey. Since then, I've been slowly learning the answer to a question I think most of us don't even know we are all asking: *am I loved?*

Recently a friend asked me a different question, "What qualifies you to write a book about being loved?" I was tempted to respond to my friend with some of my achievements. To tell him how I had excelled during my internship and was given a full-time opportunity with the same organization. How a few years later I was transferred to a larger community to grow an existing program. Then, how I received regional recognition and began training others. To tell my friend about my Masters of Divinity and ongoing interest in the Greek language of the New Testament. And finally, to tell him that since 2008 I have been working with men, helping them navigate the ups and downs of life. And if that wasn't enough for him, to tell him of all I have learned through 18 years of marriage and being a father of three and friend to many.

Isn't that how we all tend to look at ourselves and our lives? When any of us are asked the question, "Who *are* you?" we usually answer it as if we've been asked, "What do you *do*?" We respond with our job titles, the number of children we have, how long we've been in our chosen career field, where we went to college. Over the last decade, I've heard literally thousands of people from all ages and backgrounds answer the question of "Who are you?" and it's taken me a while to put my finger on what's irked me about their responses. The similarity? Everyone seems to be doubting their own worth.

You see, it's much less risky to talk about what we *do*, rather than who we *are*. What we don't realize is that by focusing on our outward achievements and milestones, we are missing God's feelings about us entirely, and ignoring the fact that our worth actually has nothing to do with what we do, how we perform, or what we achieve. The truth is: we are loved because we were designed by a creative, loving God, and we were given a specific and unique purpose on this earth. God's innate love for us is an intrinsic part of simply being human.

How do *you* answer the question, "Am I loved?" Not in your head, but on the inside, in that deeper place that is in you? What is your internal dialogue that plays on a loop in your thoughts throughout the day? Do you even know, or does it seems so normal that you just go with it?

Secondly, how do you describe yourself? It's become second nature for me to answer that question: "I am a strong, confident, warm, truthful, assertive, courageous, creative man. That's who I am. That's a far cry from how I operated for so many years believing that I was weak, fearful, distant, and tentative. That is the truth about who I am. In response to my friend's question, it's my journey of coming to understand that truth that qualifies—and inspires—me to write this book.

That's the invitation of Jesus, and the hope I have for you with this book. Let's do it together: let's learn the answer to the question, "Am I loved?" It just might change everything.

Shawn Petree
Seattle, Washington
December, 2017

A Note about Belief On-Ramps

At the end of each chapter in this book you will find a *Belief On-Ramp*. This is an opportunity for you to "do the work," so to speak, in order to make a change in your life. Sometimes you'll be invited to journal, other times to simply listen. You'll be invited to reflect and soul search. Sometimes you'll be encouraged to forgive (yourself and others), and sometimes even to repent, where necessary.

The word *repentance* is often misunderstood in our culture. The Greek word for repentance (*metanoia*) means: "re-evaluation that leads to action." Thomas Keating said it was "to rethink one's life, to change the direction you are looking for happiness."

So, the Belief On-Ramps are your chance to pause and rethink, evaluate, and consider a change in direction. I hope these are helpful for you.

I personally find it useful to keep a journal to write down my thoughts and what I sense I am hearing from the Lord. I encourage you to do the same or something similar. It helps to articulate the thoughts and have something to go back to later for refreshment or reinforcement.

And don't rush the process. To make the most of what God might be saying to you as you are working through this book, I invite you to take your time with each chapter. Maybe put the book down and take a week or two to interact with God through prayer, Scripture reading, and journaling. In the light of His Word and His love, honestly examine lies you've believed about yourself, and identify the truths you want to embrace. When you have settled on what those are, pick the book back up again and keep going. Remember, it's a journey. And I'm learning right along with you.

Chapter One

Arriving Home

I'd finally "arrived."

I was in the position I wanted at work, tasked with leading a large group of people toward a common vision. I was receiving a lot of praise for my efforts. My wife, Anna, and I were seven years into marriage, and it was going pretty well. Through some sort of miracle, we had just moved into our dream house. And after three years of trying to conceive a child we were staring at our own three-month-old daughter, Moriah. Life was playing out just as I had hoped.

Until it wasn't.

Asking the Bigger Questions

It was an opportunity at work that brought me face-to-face with my reality. I was asked to be the keynote speaker at a multi-day event that included many of my peers as well as the teams they led. I was really excited for the opportunity, and I was ready! I would be at the platform a few times each day during the event, and looked forward to the chance to influence others.

Two days into the conference, I realized I was craving feedback from people as soon as I walked off the stage. As each session ended, my desire for affirmation increased. I was desperate to hear

I was doing well—or at least okay. People did say nice things and affirmed my contribution, but it wasn't enough—not even close! By the time the event concluded, I was reeling. I felt alone, isolated, confused, and downright angry that not more people had commented on my "performance."

Yeah, that's it. That's what it was. It was a performance. I had stood in front of people on that stage, performing. Hoping. Subconsciously begging my peers to tell me I was great. But what I soon came to realize was that I was not only performing on the stage for a few days during that event, but I was performing every single day. My entire life had become a stage.

I wish I could tell you I realized my propensity to perform in that moment of clarity, quickly remedied the problem, and moved on. But that isn't how the story played out. In fact, things got worse as I returned home. Anger, depression, fear, loss of sleep, and unexplainable medical issues set in. So, I started asking questions—big questions about faith, God, the impact of past experiences, and the importance of relationships.

At the end of this rather painful season of my life, two recurring themes emerged from my reflection: the terrifying presence of Fear and Control, and the notable absence of Peace.

The One Question We Are Asking

David Richo, in his book *When Love Meets Fear*, says this about fear and control: "Wanting to be in control is another way of saying: I am afraid of having to grieve. I am afraid that if you do not give me what I want I will feel bad and I will have to grieve the loss. I do not really control to get my way as much as I do to avoid how bad I feel if I do not get my way."[1] This is a fascinating insight about the inner workings of control.

I agree that control is rooted in fear. We are simply afraid of what might happen if we don't maintain control, so we do our best to make sure that every situation produces our desired outcome. In this time of personal chaos, I realized this was what I was doing to a T: controlling people and outcomes as much as possible. I even wanted to control how people responded to my contributions to the world or their individual lives. I realized that the more I cared about someone or something, the more I tried to control the person or situation. In my pursuit of the "perfect life," I was using control as a tool to attempt to get a question answered that, at the time, I didn't even know I was asking.

In retrospect, I have come to believe it's a question we are all asking. We may not know it's the question, or that we are even asking it, but we are. And most of the time, the answer we get from our culture, from our past, from other people, is, "No."

So what's the question? It's this:

Am I loved?

It's taken me a long time, but I've learned the answer to this question and so can you.

As I reflected on this thought, I realized that for years, a recording in my head had played a script of pain and disappointment. Everything was filtered through my experience. That's when I decided to go back into my story—my life—and see where this penchant to perform and seek others' approval set in.

My story began with the six-year-old me in our living room, where my parents sat us down to inform us they had decided to no longer be married. The scene is full of confusion and sadness. Even though I was there with my three-year-old brother and seven-year-old sister, I felt very afraid and alone. Maybe that is when fear set in for me, fear that eventually led to control.

As I considered this possibility I decided to investigate the opposite of fear: faith. Belief. Specifically, I chose to pick up my Bible and, over a five-month span, read the four Gospels, carefully looking for any story that involved faith or belief. What I discovered was astounding!

Discovering Belief

I began my quest by reading Chapter 1 of each Gospel (Matthew, Mark, Luke, and John) on different days and pausing to journal each time I ran across the words "faith," "belief," or "unbelief." After that, I went to Chapter 2 of each book and so on. There was no time goal . . . it was private time with the Father.

Each morning, when I came across a statement about belief or unbelief, I'd stop and note what I was hearing and feeling. Often it would take two or three days to get through a single chapter. (This did not sit well with my internal wiring. My nature is more about results than pondering.) Somehow, though, there was no hurry to complete this task, and learning about faith became more important than checking a chapter off the list.

During my first week of reading, one of Jesus' statements jumped out at me. In Mark 1:15, Jesus says, "Believe in the gospel."(NASB) I hadn't noticed that before. Exactly what, I wondered, was Jesus inviting people into with this statement? As I continued to read, day after day, it was amazing to observe the weight Jesus allowed "belief" to play in different people's lives, and even His own life. In fact, in many of the stories I read about Jesus, I saw He was allowing belief to dictate the outcome of peoples' lives!

I found in Mark 5, for example, a poignant account of belief. In fact, if you have a Bible, I encourage you to take a look at it right now. You'll see multiple people who end up at the feet of Jesus.

The first story involves a sick girl and a desperate father named Jairus—a man whose level of belief is incredibly inspiring and challenging to me. This father said to Jesus, "Please come and lay your hands on (my daughter) so she *will get well* and live" (Mark 5:23, NASB, emphasis mine).

But by the time Jesus got around to going to heal this man's daughter, Jairus' friends came to him and said, "Your daughter has died; why trouble the teacher anymore" (vs. 35)?

Jesus, overhearing their words, told Jairus, "Do not be afraid any longer, only *believe*" (vs. 36). Just before Jesus honored Jairus' belief and healed his daughter, He did one other significant thing: He got unbelief out of the room (v. 40). He literally made sure everyone who didn't believe that He could raise the girl was shown the door. Once the environment was right, Jesus took the hand of the little girl and she got up!

Ironically, this story is punctuated by another incident involving belief. (These people were coming out of the woodwork!) On the way to Jairus' house, Jesus found himself in the midst of a large crowd, where He encountered a woman with a hemorrhage. When this woman heard about Jesus, her first thought was one of belief: "If I can just touch his garments, I will get well" (Mark 5:28, NASB). So she made her way in (and by "in" I mean she crawled to Jesus) and did what her belief compelled her to do—she reached out and touched the hem of His robe. Now, this went entirely against all Jewish law and convention—a woman with this kind of issue was considered "unclean" and could not be touched. Not only was this an act of belief, it was an incredible act of courage!

Immediately, Jesus felt power go out of Him. He looked about and noticed this woman on her knees. Even He was taken back by this kind of belief! His statement to her was, "Daughter, *your faith* has made you well; go in peace and be healed of your affliction" (v.34, emphasis mine).

Over and over again, I observed a pattern in the Gospels of folks hitting their knees when they encountered Jesus. It seems they took this posture for one of two reasons: respect or desperation. Part of the reason I know this is, well . . . I've been there! In the story I opened this chapter with, I was in desperation after that disastrous speaking engagement trip. I needed something and had no idea what it was. I was in crisis.

I thought, *How could this be happening?* I had been "saved" at a young age. At the time, it seemed simple. From my perspective, all I had to do was be better than the kids around me and Jesus would love me more than them. (That was the interpretation my adolescent mind conjured up, anyway.) So that's what I did. I made better choices than other kids, stayed out of trouble, and said my prayers at night. I sang the words to the song "Jesus Loves Me" often.

However, in hindsight, I now realize the words I was saying to myself were, *Do you really think you measure up? Don't take yourself so seriously . . . you'll never find someone to love you. You're quite a mess, you know. You probably ought to work out more . . . you probably ought to study harder . . . you'll never amount to much . . . look at you!*

I began to realize I'd been shackled with fear and unbelief most of my life. In this time of personal chaos and despair, I became aware of a choice I needed to make. Would I allow fear to continue its destructive dominance in my life, or would I walk through it with Jesus and find healing in Him?

Coming to My Senses

There is a story of a young man in the Bible who finds himself in a similar place in his life. He too, has a choice to make. And because of that key moment in my own life, I could relate to this young man's loneliness. Jesus told us his story:

Once there was a man who had two sons. The younger one said to his father, "Father, give me my share of the property that will come to me." So he divided up his property between the two of them.

Before very long, the younger son collected all his belongings and went off to a foreign land, where he squandered his wealth in the wildest extravagance. And when he had run through all his money, a terrible famine arose in that country, and he began to feel the pinch. Then he went and hired himself out to one of the citizens of that country who sent him out into the fields to feed the pigs. He got to the point of longing to stuff himself with the food the pigs were eating and not a soul gave him anything. (Luke 15:11-16, Phillips)

After demanding his inheritance from his father (something that would have been unthinkable in the Jewish culture), the son in the story leaves home and spends all of his money on wild living. His money runs out, and he eventually gets hired on with a pig farmer, possibly the most humiliating job possible for a Jewish son. In the midst of personal turmoil, something important happens to this young man: *he gets to the point* of longing to stuff himself with the food the pigs are eating (vs. 16, emphasis added). From privilege and wealth to poverty and pig slop. Young's Literal Translation phrases "He got to the point" this way: "And having come to himself . . ."

I like to think that this young man comes to the end of himself and realizes something must change. That's what happened to me. I got to the point where life wasn't working. Anxiety, fear, control, and feeling alone are examples of life not working. The son in the story makes an important decision, and so did I.

The story continues:

Then he (the young son) came to his senses and cried aloud, "Why, dozens of my father's hired men have got more food

*than they can eat and here I am dying of hunger! I will get up
and go back to my father, and I will say to him, 'Father, I have
done wrong in the sight of Heaven and in your eyes. I don't
deserve to be called your son any more. Please take me on as one
of your hired men.'" (Luke 15:17-19, Phillips)*

As I imagine this young man, desperate and out of options,
feeling at the end of himself, I wonder if he ran scenarios through
his head the way I do. I often think, *Okay, this isn't working; I wonder if this other thing would. Surely if I do that it will help the situation.* It rarely does.

Returning to the son's story, it seems like the options that
came up in his list of scenarios went something like this, *Oh, I've
got it! I'll get up and go back to my father . . . that's what I'll do. I'll
prepare a speech and go. That's a great idea!* Jesus, as the narrator of
the story, says this about the son: "So he got up and went to his
father" (v. 20, Phillips). There it is, action. Re-evaluation of life that
leads to action. The son doesn't just come up with the idea to go
to the father, or consider it enough that he knows it would be best
for him to go to the father. No, this son actually gets up and goes.

When I hit the crisis revealed through my speaking engagement, I, too, had a decision to make after I'd run my scenarios. I
decided to get up and go to the Father.

If you are not familiar with how this story ends, I highly recommend you read the conclusion in Luke 15. It's remarkable, to
say the least, how this young man "comes to his senses" (vs. 17),
gets up, and goes to his father. In the pages that follow, you will
read how I (and others) also "got up and went to the Father." In
the process, we each came to know the answer to the question, *Am
I loved?*

But it was more than that. We didn't simply receive the answer.
We have learned to *believe the truth* that we are loved.

> *I have no greater joy than to hear that my*
> *children are walking in the truth.*
> *3 John 1:2, NIV*

✦ Belief On-Ramp #1 ✦

The son in Jesus' story *longed* to stuff himself with pig slop, but he knew that, even in his deep hunger, the food would not satisfy. The same is true for us. Only one thing curbs our longing, and it's actually not a thing at all; it's a return to the Father.

You have read a little of my story, and some of the story of the young man in Luke 15. Now take some time for yourself, at least an hour if you can. Here are a few questions/thoughts to consider:

- ✦ How do you feel today? (e.g., overwhelmed, confused, great, unfulfilled, lonely)
- ✦ Complete the following: I tend to try to control my environment or others around me when (circle your answer):

I often / sometimes / rarely seek
approval from others.

(If sometimes or often, why do you think this is?)

- ✦ Have you had a significant moment in your life that caused you to consider the deeper questions of life? If so, how has this changed the way you live?
- ✦ What is one thing you have a hard time believing could ever change in your life?

Chapter Two

Redefining Belief

For years, I thought I knew what it meant to believe. I had it all figured out. After all, in the culture in which I grew up, "belief" in Jesus was a one-time event that could be talked about, remembered, and celebrated. I've come to realize it's not that simple.

Critical moments of "belief" can happen in people's lives in various ways and at various times. Sometimes a moment of belief can be "pivotal" (directional) in a person's life, and sometimes a moment of belief is a "pinnacle" (emotional) event. But whether we experience belief in God (and His love, His involvement in our life, His goodness, etc.) logically or emotionally (both are important), what we actually *do* with that belief makes all the difference in the world.

Belief Defined

Expanding our definition of "belief" may help explain what I mean by this. What does it mean to believe? Most people, regardless of what they think about Him personally, will admit that someone named Jesus walked the earth 2,000 years ago. They may also acknowledge that Jesus' teachings have had an incredible impact on an enormous number of people since then. It is entirely possible to believe that Jesus existed without believing in who He claimed to be or in what He taught.

What did Jesus teach that had such a lasting effect on the world? In the first account we have of Jesus speaking to people, He says, "The time has come at last—the kingdom of God has arrived. You must change your hearts and minds and *believe* the good news." (Mark 1:15 NASB, emphasis added). The Greek word translated here as "belief" is *pisteúo*. It is understood as "to think to be true, to be persuaded of, place confidence in, to entrust a thing to another." Based on this definition, what Jesus referred to as "belief" is not a one-time event or a historical fact that can be objectively documented. Belief can apply to a particular situation, but in order for someone to believe a certain thing is true, there needs to be a level of confidence that it *actually is* true.

Not only was Jesus' first message about "believing," but He maintained that simple message throughout His teachings. He often asked people to believe, and He commended belief over and over when He saw it in action. One example is in Matthew 9, where we see the word in its various forms:

> *As Jesus went on from there, two blind men followed him, calling out, "Have mercy on us, Son of David!"*
>
> *When he had gone indoors, the blind men came to him, and he asked them, "Do you believe [pisteúo] that I am able to do this?"*
>
> *"Yes, Lord," they replied.*
>
> *Then he touched their eyes and said, "According to your faith [pistis] let it be done to you;" and their sight was restored. (Matthew 9:27-30, NASB)*

I came across the account of this encounter between Jesus and these two blind men during a time when I was stuck in fear and depression. After reading it, I thought of what I would say if I'd called out for help with my depression and fear. I felt as if Jesus were asking me personally, "Do you believe that I am able to do this?"

I knew what my answer would be: "NO." And if I were being completely honest, my answer would be, "No, I don't really believe that you can do this, God, so I am going to do it myself. I am in control." That day, I realized that if my life was going to change, and if I wanted any chance at a future apart from worry, fear, and anxiety, then I would have to learn what it meant to *really* believe.

What if, in fact, the result of "believing" is also to believe that God can do this, whatever the "this" is we are currently facing? What if the goal is to move beyond living in our heads, beyond having everything figured out? What if belief goes way beyond a one-time event? What if it is, instead, something that is cultivated as we release control and learn to surrender our lives to the one who is "able to do this?"

As I read this story of the blind men over and over again, it dawned on me that there are two "this-es'" Jesus is referring to. One is situational; Jesus is asking the two blind men if they believe He can make them see again. The second "this" is broader. It's a question Jesus asks each of us, a question of belief in the person of Jesus. Do these two blind men believe that Jesus is for them? Do you and I believe that He is for us? Do we believe He is with us in every instance throughout the day and that He deeply cares?

Believing Before It Happens

Soon after I read the story of Jesus with the blind men, I had an opportunity to put this new perspective of belief into action. It happened one summer when my wife Anna and I gathered our little crew and boarded a big airplane to meet up with the Texas side of our family. During one of our days there, we ventured out to Six Flags Fiesta Texas. My siblings and I had enjoyed the Six Flags theme parks as children, and we were excited for the next generation to have a similar experience.

Being that our professional lives keep us busy on most days, we all committed to leaving our phones in the car. This was family time, a laid-back reprieve, free of the temptation to sneak in an email or check voicemails while standing in ride lines. This was going to be an epic day! We eagerly anticipated a day of creating memories and catching up with one another.

And so it was, until we noticed that our daughter Moriah, who was four years old at the time, was suddenly gone! We started looking around, and the first few minutes were somewhat calm. However, panic quickly began to grip us. The worst-case scenario took center stage in my mind, and I bolted for the exit, determined that if someone was trying to take her out of the park, they were going to meet the scrappy linebacker in me. The rest of the adults in our family were frantically scouring the park, searching, calling her name . . . "MORIAH!" . . . hoping . . . praying . . .

Of course, phones would have been handy at this point, because we had no way to communicate with one another. It was more than maddening! I still have to fight back the tears when I think about it. There we were, each in our own little nightmares, frantic as 10 minutes went by, then 20 minutes, and 30 minutes, with no sign of our daughter.

Standing at that exit is forever etched in my brain. As if it happened earlier today, I can remember feeling helpless as I scanned the crowd for our little girl. All I could do was breathe deeply and say, "Lord, I believe *You* can do this." In that moment, I was broken and desperate and had to will myself to believe. As I poured my eyes over every face that passed me, I kept saying over and over, "Lord, I believe You can do this."

There I was, faced with my own two-sided question for Jesus. Did I believe He could return Moriah safely? Did I believe He was for me and with me in the midst of my fear of losing my daughter, and that no matter the outcome, He would still be there?

It was 45 minutes from the time we lost Moriah to the time I got the news from a gate attendant that she had been found. The words of Jesus in John 14:1 were a comfort to me that day: "Do not let your heart be troubled; believe in God, believe also in Me."

Jesus taught us that belief keeps our heart from being overwhelmed by trouble. Oh, believe me, my heart was troubled, but the conviction that God could reunite us with Moriah, and that He was with us throughout that unknown situation, overshadowed the trouble in my heart that day. The reunion with Moriah was very emotional. Seeing her face as I ran to embrace her, having her arms wrapped around my neck as she voiced the word "Daddy," was almost more relief and happiness than I could bear.

I learned something about belief that day. I learned that belief is not a one-time decision, and it is not about outcomes or results. It is instead about trusting that God can do "this," whatever the "this" is in front of us in the moment. It's about believing that He is with us, real time, and we are not on our own.

But there is yet another aspect of belief that goes even deeper than a situation or reality that we are not alone. If you will humor me and allow me to "geek out" on the Greek text of one verse of Scripture, we may be able to get a better grasp of what Jesus was ultimately getting at with His first message about belief.

Learning to Believe

There is a prayer recorded in the New Testament book of Ephesians that many people consider to be the goal or hope for those who desire to live the life Jesus promised in His teachings. This prayer is only fully realized in the Greek text. We're used to seeing it in English like this: ". . . so that Christ may dwell in your hearts through faith" (Ephesians 3:17, NASB).

But our English translations miss it. Here is that portion from a translation that attempts to capture the intent of the original Greek: ". . . that Christ might finally settle down and feel completely at home in your hearts through your faith." This remarkable image from Kenneth Wuest's Expanded Translation really helps the implications of this verse make sense to me. Christ, settling down and feeling completely at home inside of me, inside of you.

The whole verse has incredible implications, but a few things specifically stand out. *Kardia,* "heart" as translated in English, is better explained as "the inmost being or inner self." It is what controls the mind, emotions, and will. Many of us have been taught about a one-time decision of belief to "receive Jesus into our hearts." However, this prayer in Ephesians explains the real goal: Christ feeling completely at home in our inmost being. He wants to feel completely at home in us, but He needs full access. So often we only want to give Him parts of ourselves or sections of our life. He wants everything; His desire is complete surrender.

But honestly, how is that even possible? That question is answered with Jesus' next statement: "through your faith." There's that word *pisteou,* or "belief," again. That could easily say, "through your belief in the truth."

Part of this truth is the confidence that *I am loved* (you too). It's the truth that God is crazy about us, and can't stop thinking about us. He's always pursuing, ever engaging, infinitely forgiving, unfailingly kind, patient, and gracious. That is the truth! Here, then, is the full way we can understand Ephesians 3:17: *So that Christ might finally settle down and feel completely at home in your* **innermost being** *through your* **belief in the truth** *(that you are loved).*

The prayer suggests that the settling down of Jesus in our inmost being happens through our belief in the truth about who He is and what He came to do for us. The truth about me and about you is the same: we are loved by the One who created us. This is the ultimate understanding of belief lived out—living today believing that what God says about us it true.

Belief Lived Out

When my friend Marvin began to believe this, everything—I mean everything—changed for him. Along with his wife Jeanett, Marvin is the co-founder of Divine Alternatives for Dads Services, an organization dedicated to restoring absent fathers with their children by helping men navigate the relational and legal barriers that hold them back. Marvin entered into this work to help men in the same position he had once been in, and the journey he himself had successfully navigated in reconnecting with his children after many years on drugs and on the streets.

Now an accomplished and respected community leader and committed follower of Jesus, Marvin has a unique perspective on belief. He said to me, "Shawn, I had faith. My faith was in the dopeman! I believed the dopeman would be there when I rolled by to get the goods. I had no reason to question that fact. I was good to him, bringing him the cash, and he was good to me, giving me the product." Marvin went on to say, "Once I decided to believe in Jesus and allow that to impact my life, I realized that all I had to do was *flip the faith*. I began to transfer my belief in the destructive things in my life to belief that God was for me and was with me."

To comprehend the extent of the "flip the faith" in Marvin's life, it's helpful to understand where he came from. In his book, *Becoming DADS: A Mission to Restore Absent Fathers*,[2] we learn what that looked like:

At 43 years old his life was going nowhere and he (Marvin) didn't know what to do or where to go. He felt utterly lost and totally alone. As he wandered back into his girlfriend's apartment he was greeted by what seeemed like all he ever heard now . . . more bad news.

"I'm pregnant again," she told him sadly. The man thought to himself, "One child just born and now another on its way?" He felt a sharp pain in the pit of his stomach. The only money coming in was the little bit he earned as a day laborer and the $1,000 or so he could get from a government tax refund check. What he had before thought of as "always new"—going from job to job, smoking crack with his girlfriend to escape his pain—was getting really old.

He had six children scattered throughout the Seattle foster care system and elsewhere. Now there would be another, this one coming into a crack environment. Deep down, he knew they could not raise this child in any sort of healthy way.

He had started smoking crack regularly with his new girlfriend and her friends to make himself feel better, priding himself that he wasn't an "addict" like them—as if his drug use were under control. In reality he was just as trapped in addiction as they were. At the root he was seeking to numb the pain he felt. His children were being raised by strangers. He was passing on to them, in all of their innocence, the very curse he had inherited. This cut him deep to the core.

How had he come to this place? He was overwhelmed by the consequences of years of making bad choices that had seemed to make sense at the time. He felt trapped by single fatherhood and a doomed sense of unfulfilled responsibility. He was entangled in his addiction and the confusing web it had woven around his life and his identity. Now there seemed no

*way out. It felt like he was being sucked down a whirling fun-
nel; it just spun faster and faster, dragging him into its vortex,
and he was helpless to get out.*

Marvin says he reached a pivotal moment when he went to see
a pastor to talk about taking steps to grow his faith. The pastor told
him that God's invitation was to rely on Him for everything. He
told Marvin that the primary way to grow in faith is to invest in a
personal relationship with Jesus. Marvin's reply? "Shoot, I haven't
ever trusted anyone with a relationship!"

Despite this reality, Marvin decided that his pain, and his
family's pain, was deep enough that he was willing to *believe*, and
to risk putting his trust in a growing relationship with Jesus. Marvin embraced both aspects of belief that I've talked about in this
chapter: he believed God could bring about transformation in his
life and family, and he also believed God loved him and would be
with him in the process.

Marvin has been walking in this relationship with God for
more than twenty years and proving it to be true. Along the way,
he married his then-girlfriend, Jeanett, and has been reunited with
his eight children. Over the past 20-plus years, Marvin and Jeanett
have helped hundreds of men reconnect with their families and
become contributing members of society. In turn, many men have
also learned to believe—and experience—the transforming Father
love of God.

Marvin's pivotal experience of belief was the catalyst for
him to truly understand that he was marvelously loved by God.
It resulted in his living out that belief by investing the love he
had received into hundreds and even thousands of other people
who desperately needed to experience that same truth. This is the
power of "belief."

> *As a father has compassion on his children,*
> *so the Lord has compassion on those who*
> *fear him;*
> *for he knows how we are formed, he*
> *remembers that we are dust.*
> *Psalm 103: 3-4, NIV*

✦ Belief On-Ramp #2 ✦

I want you to get away for an hour unplugged. Yes, actually turn off your phone or leave it in your car and go sit somewhere. (Make sure people know where you are; I mean, don't scare anyone or anything. Our experience losing Moriah at the theme park and not having a phone with us does remind us to always have a plan for emergencies! But unplugging from life from time to time is too important to not do it.)

Here's what you can do during your "unplugged" time:

Read Matthew 9:27-30. Pause for two minutes.
Read it again. Pause for two minutes.
Read it again. Pause for two minutes.
Read it again.

Now, think about your life and how you go about your days. Is there anything troubling you right now? Anything that is causing doubt, fear, or worry? If so, what is your answer to Jesus' question: "Do you believe that I am able to do this?"

Chapter Three

Exposing Lies

In the process of beginning to learn what "belief" really means, I decided to explore the opposite of belief, which is fear. Where might fear and anxiety have come into my story?

I knew without even having to think twice about it. The scene was the living room of my childhood home. I was seven years old, sitting there with my nine-year-old sister and four-year-old brother. Even as I write these words, I can see our couch, a lamp on the table beside it, and the entrance into the kitchen. That room already had undesirable memories for me, as it was the place where our parents had sat us down nine months earlier to tell us that they were no longer going to be married. Our mother had primary custody of us, so it was the four of us in the living room on this particular night, a night forever etched in my memory.

We had just returned home from my tee ball game and I was standing next to a chair in my brown and green baseball uniform. My brother and sister were sitting on the couch with our mom when strange words came out of her mouth. "Kids, I believe it is best if I leave town and don't see you again." There's not much I remember after that statement, apart from the crying and begging her to stay.

While I may not remember what else happened in the moments following my mom's statement to us, I now realize as a man how that moment caused me to believe some things about myself that were not true. This happens to a lot of us. Not this specific scene, but a scene or multiple memories that invite us to believe a lie instead of the truth about who we are. Being able to identify events in our past that have had a profound impact on how we see ourselves is one thing. However, creating time and space to get at these lies and replace them with truth is an important step in learning to really believe who God is, what is true about us, and that we are completely and fundamentally loved.

Encountering Truth

You might question the importance of dealing with this kind of thing (our belief system). After all, most people go their whole lives without going through a process of "identifying lies" or doing anything to attempt to change what they believe about themselves, or about God. As I considered this for myself, I looked with fresh eyes at an encounter Jesus had that showed me what can happen when a person accepts the invitation of Jesus to tell the truth.

The scene finds Jesus at a community well, tired from traveling and wanting a drink. He meets a woman who is at this well alone, getting water for her household. (We learn later in the story that she's had multiple extra-marital affairs, which was very much looked down on in that culture, to put it mildly!) I wonder what this woman thought about herself as she made her way to get water at the well by herself that day. Did she feel unworthy to give and receive love? Maybe that's why she kept turning to one relationship after another—she was trying to fulfill her life. Whatever her inner motivations, God brought her to an encounter with Jesus to show His love to her. Jesus is the truth; when people encounter Him, they encounter truth.

When Jesus meets this woman at the well, she has a number of questions for Him. Eventually, Jesus tells her of another kind of water available to her that will cause her to never thirst again. Instead of responding with skepticism or unbelief, she replies, "Sir, give me this water so that I won't get thirsty and have to keep coming here to draw water" (John 4:15, NIV).

In order to make this statement to Jesus, the woman must have some hope that the water is actually available. But before Jesus gives her water, He asks her about her past and the way she is living. Check out what this woman does; she tells the truth!

> *"I haven't got a husband!" the woman answered.*
>
> *"You are quite right in saying, 'I haven't got a husband,'" replied Jesus, "for you have had five husbands and the man you have now is not your husband at all. Yes, you spoke the simple truth when you said that." (vv. 17–18, NIV)*

When we encounter Jesus in truth, we can trust that He will expose us without shaming us. This was the experience of the woman at the well. The story goes on: she tells Jesus the truth about how she is living, and takes Him up on His offer of living water. She leaves her water jar behind and goes into town to tell the people about this one who could be the Messiah. I love her simple message: "Come and see a man that told me everything I ever did" . . . *and loves me anyway* (v. 29, my emphasis).

There is a good chance that many of the people in the town knew this woman's story. When she showed up to tell them about a man who loved and accepted her just as she was, their interest was piqued. The account goes on to tell us, "Many of the Samaritans from that town believed in Him because of the woman's testimony" (v. 39).

Did you catch that? Many of the townspeople believed *because of the woman's belief.* There is a chain reaction going on here, and the results are astounding! Belief inspires belief, which results in more belief.

The best part of the story is the transformation that takes place at the end of the encounter. Jesus shows back up on the scene and interacts directly with the people. The story ends with, "We no longer believe because of what you (the woman) said; now we have heard for ourselves, and we know that this man really is the Savior of the world" (v. 42, NIV).

The woman Jesus met at the well that day experienced a profound change in her life once she encountered the truth of Jesus. We don't know what specific lies she was believing before she met Jesus, but we can see from the story that her encounter with Jesus led to a profoundly different life for this woman and for her community. Whatever lies she was believing about herself, whatever fears she had that compelled her into the lifestyle she was living, were replaced by the truth of what Jesus thought about her, and belief in His love for her.

Lies Revealed

A similar experience happened for me when I came to recognize and understand the lies I had come to believe about myself. The scene was not a well in a Middle Eastern desert village. For me, it was a bluff overlooking the Guemes Channel in the San Juan Islands of Washington State.

When I moved from Texas to the Pacific Northwest, I knew I needed a place to get away regularly. Growing up in West Texas, we were close enough to Colorado to experience amazing backpacking and outdoor adventure on a regular basis. The San Juan

Islands, two hours north of Seattle, became my place to get away when I needed time to retreat, and space to process life.

When I hit my low point of fear and anxiety, I knew I needed to get away. Thankfully, my friend Ryan was up for taking a kayaking trip with me on short notice. My wife recognized I was in a bad place and was more than happy to send us out. I knew it was time to create an opportunity to ask God about the depth of my fear and unbelief in all areas of life.

Slowly, over the three days Ryan and I were away, through prayer, journaling, self-reflection, and conversation, the core lies I believed about myself surfaced. I realized there were three core lies I'd believed most of my life.

First, I realized that, for a long time, I had been believing the lie that at some point everyone was going to leave and I would be left alone. Because of my past, I was living my adult life as if the story of my upbringing was going to be replayed over and over. Put simply: it was the fear of abandonment that came into the light.

The second lie that surfaced surprised me a bit. I was living a strange lie that I was a boy, not a man. That may sound a bit odd so let me unpack it. A boy looks for safety and security, expecting others to create it. A man creates safety and security and invites others into it. I didn't feel like I could handle many of the situations I encountered on a day-to-day basis. When I met these situations I felt like a boy, ill equipped to handle what was in front of me.

The final lie was exposed as I sat on the bluff overlooking Guemes Channel. Enjoying the serenity of that beautiful vista, I realized there was a deep conviction that I wouldn't ever be fully free or at peace. The line of thinking I'd been caught up in was that my life could only be "okay." There was something in me that believed I could only *manage* the fear, anxiety, and depression that shook me at times. In my mind, a life at peace with God and others, even with myself, was not attainable.

As we paddled and camped, these lies continued to surface. I knew something had to be done about them that weekend, right there in the Islands. When Sunday morning rolled around, with journal in hand, Ryan and I made our way to the other side of the island, ending up on another bluff right over the water. As we walked, the battle raged. A full frontal assault was launched from a coterie of fear, dread, and shame, flinging accusations of indignity and offers of solace if I were only to go back into hiding. It was hell in my head that morning. Thankfully, mercy reigned.

Ryan, I would soon discover, was the perfect man to be with that morning. He didn't know what was about to go down, but my soul was about to be laid bare and I needed a courageous friend to be in this with me. As I opened up about the lies that God the Father had revealed, Ryan leaned in and we prayed through each lie in an effort to break this cycle of fear and unbelief.

It took guts to do this, but there was something about saying this out loud in front of a trusted friend that made it very transactional. "Ryan," I said, "God has shown me this weekend some things deep inside me that go way back into my past. I've discovered that I've been believing some lies I didn't even know were in me. Check out this list of things that have surfaced: I'm a boy, and I'm scared. My heart is bad; I won't ever be well. I am a victim and will always be a victim. No one really cares." Next I read the three core lies I had identified on our adventure.

"Would you be willing to pray through these?" Ryan asked me.

I wanted to say "No," but knew that it was time.

"Sure," I said. "What do I do?"

Ryan said, "Bro, I don't know. Just try saying something like: 'God, I realize I've been believing the lie that . . .' And then ask God what the truth is."

So I started. "God, I realize I've been believing the lie that people are going to leave me at any time. It's made me live as if my wife will leave me, and as if all my friends will leave me. I've even left people first, so they wouldn't get the chance to hurt me. I confess that this is a lie; people won't always leave me. I don't want to live this way anymore." As soon as I finished exposing this first lie, a verse came into my head: "So be strong and courageous! Do not be afraid and do not panic before them. For the LORD your God will personally go ahead of you. He will neither fail you nor abandon you" (Deuteronomy 31:6, NLT).

Ryan and I went on to pray through the remaining lies I'd identified. For the most part, we had no idea what we were doing, but God led us through breaking these lies in my life. We put a stake in the ground that morning on Saddlebag Island. The lies were broken and I left that experience changed, just like that woman at the well.

Freedom from Bondage

When I got back from that kayaking trip, I'd done the key work of identifying and dealing with those lies. I felt a sense of relief for having done so. The darkness didn't seem quite as dark as before I left. But I knew that one weekend wasn't just going to erase all the years of living under those lies. After all, the hope is not to simply identify and replace lies with truth, but to move closer to actually living in the reality that we are loved. I needed to walk out of the lies I believed and into the truth.

I had to be honest and admit that I harbored a lot of anger and bitterness toward my mom for leaving when I was young. That anger and bitterness was keeping me trapped in the lies and unable to fully accept the embrace God had for me. This led to yet another key scenario—not the living room where I sat at age seven with my siblings, but this time the kitchen of my own home twenty years later.

On that day, I picked up the phone and called my mother to ask for forgiveness for holding bitterness and hatred toward her for so many years. She was taken aback, but I knew it was the right thing to do. And something incredible happened through that night, through that phone conversation. I felt immense relief . . . and so did she!

My mom and I started over in our relationship that evening on the phone, and we maintained a relationship until her last day on Earth. I learned more of the story of my mom's childhood— and it was horrendous. Both of her parents were heavily addicted to alcohol. Abuse, neglect, malnutrition, and an overwhelming sense of fear were my mom's daily reality.

I remember her wiping back the tears as she told me a story from her early childhood. She recalled climbing up the cabinets and onto the counter one morning, looking for something to eat in the upper cupboard. Her parents were checked out and hungover, and she was desperate. There was nothing to eat except a can of Crisco, and she actually pulled a spoon out of the drawer and ate a spoonful, just to satisfy the intense hunger she felt. As I listened to my mom tell this story (and many others like this) from her childhood, my compassion for her grew.

As you might imagine, my mom carried incredible guilt, shame, and unforgiveness toward herself because of her decision to leave her children. In my adulthood, I began to realize the depth of pain in which my mom was living when she sat her three kids down to tell us that she was leaving. At that point in her life, my mom believed so many lies about herself that she couldn't fathom the possibility that she was the best thing for her children. Broken mothers and fathers often break their children. It's a natural consequence of pain; it gets passed on to the next generation.

However, as I began to see the positive changes in my own life through exposing lies, I had a chance to walk with my mom as she gradually left behind some of her own lies.

It's amazing what happens when we are honest with ourselves and face events from our past head on. The most effective way to get to the root of these issues is to make the time and space to do so. Whether it is a weekend trip, a day away unplugged from the world, or an early morning in the comforts of our own home, giving time and space for God to reveal these lies can be a critical tool in learning to believe the truth that we are loved by Him.

> *It is for freedom that Christ has set us free.*
> *Stand firm, then, and do not let yourselves*
> *be burdened again by a yoke of slavery.*
> *Galatians 5:1, NIV*

✦ Belief On-Ramp # 3 ✦

For this one, set aside a minimum of four hours, again, unplugged if possible.

Begin by going through your life in 10-year increments. (Allow 15 to 20 minutes per increment.) Identify any core memories or consistent messages from others you remember hearing during that increment of time that might have developed into a lie you still tell yourself subconsciously (e.g., *I'm too small, too big, can't do anything right, always in trouble, won't amount to anything, not worth my parents' time, bossy, difficult to get along with,* etc.). Write down anything that comes to mind.

Look over the list of possible lies and identify any themes (20-30 minutes). Write about potential lies that come to mind.

Be as honest with yourself as you can about the possible lies you may believe today. Go through a typical day/week in your current life and try to identify when you consistently get down, frustrated, or are particularly hard on yourself (20 to 30 minutes). List anything that comes to mind.

Now look over your various lists and notes and write out the top three lies you might be believing. As you read these words or statements about yourself, do they resonate?

Take these lies to God. Admit that you have believed these things about yourself. Ask Him to free you of them. Finally, turn each of these lies into an "I no longer . . ." statement (e.g., *I no longer believe that everyone will eventually leave me*).

Thank the Lord for the freedom that is yours through Christ Jesus, and ask Him to fill you with His Spirit, to live out the opposite of these lies—and the truth that *you are loved.*

Chapter Four

Believing the Truth About Ourselves

It's one thing to *expose* the lies we've been believing about ourselves throughout our lives; it's another thing altogether to *do something* about them. The really life-changing work happens through replacing those lies with truth.

At the end of the kayak adventure with my friend Ryan, I decided to be honest with myself about the messages that were running in my conscious and subconscious mind throughout most days. I took some time and wrote down the words and phrases that described my internal dialogue. The first words that came to mind were *scared* and *afraid*. Then, *worried*. Then a realization that I would, at times, bend the truth in hopes that others would approve of me.

Next, I admitted to myself that I performed for others and cared a lot about what others thought of me. After that, the painful descriptive word *weak*. Through this process, it also came to light that I would often hang back and not take initiative. Then the kicker, just one word: *fearful*.

Once I got these specific words out on paper in my journal, I laid them in front of me and had a very practical conversation with God. Although I had been following Jesus for a while, this type of frank conversation with the Father was somewhat new to me.

It went something like this: "God, thank you for revealing these deep lies I've believed about myself for many years. Only You fully know when each of these lies set in. I don't want to live like this anymore. I know these lies are not from You, God. Show me a way out of this pain."

After I sat in silence for a few moments, staring at this page in my journal with so many painful lies scribbled out, an idea came to me that I believe was from God. What if I wrote down the opposite of each lie? To take it a step further, I wondered what would happen if I awoke each morning and read aloud these descriptive words—words that were the opposite of what I currently believed about myself. It could be powerful!

So that's exactly what I did. I have read this statement every morning since I wrote it in my journal so many years ago. It has become a daily declaration for me. Over the years, as the Holy Spirit has continued to reveal to me new truths about myself, I have tweaked the prayer. This is what I read each morning about who I am:

My name is Shawn Raymond Petree, Beloved,
I am loved.
I am Your chosen son. I am family.
Your Spirit is in me. Jesus is formed
(and is forming) in me.
I am an heir of Your Kingdom, a prince, a saint.
I choose joy today!
I am a strong, confident, warm, truthful, assertive,
creative, courageous man; a warrior.
Husband to a beautiful, godly wife.
Father to three provided children.
Friend to many.
I am loved.

I want to share a little about these truths in my "Personal Declaration." Many of the words have specific meaning to me:

Raymond: I list my middle name because my granddad, *Raymond* Petree, is still my greatest hero. He loved Jesus, loved people, and loved me. His life inspires me each day.

Beloved: Most days I write in my journal, and years ago I began signing "Beloved" at the end of each entry as a reminder of who I am.

A prince: I am a son of the King, therefore a prince.

A saint: I believe the Scriptures affirm that I am a saint who sins and not a sinner at my core.

I choose joy today: I believe joy is a choice and I remind myself each day that I can choose joy, despite my circumstances today.

Each of the descriptive words I use is specifically speaking against one of the lies I once believed about myself:

Strong: For many years I believed I was weak. I specifically speak against that lie with the proclamation that *I am strong*.

Confident: I was timid and unsure, afraid to make decisions and trust. As I looked further into the word confident, I realized that it in the Latin it is *con* (with) . . . (faith)

Warm: I was often stoic and operated most of the time in "get it done" mode. During this season of discovery of lies in my life, a friend came into my office with a personal problem. He wanted to share it with me and get my thoughts. I remember thinking, "I wish he would finish sharing so that I can get some work done." This was a wake-up call for me.

Truthful: I would stretch the truth in order to be accepted by others or avoid conflict at work or at home. I told myself that it wasn't really lying as much as it was protecting others.

Assertive: I found myself often deferring to others to make decisions. Even though I was in a place of leadership at work and in a place of co-leadership with my wife at home, I was too compliant or hesitant even when I believed I knew the right decision to make.

Creative: As a Type-A, hard charging, left-brained thinker, I had convinced myself that I was not creative. Julie Cameron in her book *The Artist's Way* helped me see that I am creative. She says, "Those who speak in spiritual terms routinely refer to God as creator but seldom see 'creator' as the literal term for 'artist.' I am suggesting you take the term 'creator' quite literally. You are seeking to forge a creative alliance, artist-to-artist, with the Great Creator. Accepting this concept can greatly expand your creative possibilities."

Courageous: When I first wrote this daily declaration, I was full of fear. I knew I wanted the fear and anxiety in my life to subside, but I didn't know how to get it to go away. Declaring each day that I am courageous helped me believe the truth about who I really am.

Man: (The last of the descriptive words that specifically combated a lie.) Put simply, even though I was in my early thirties at the time, I believed at my core that I was a boy and not a man.

Husband to a beautiful, godly wife: This reminds me of the truth about my amazing wife. She is beautiful and God is in her in so many ways.

Father to three provided children: This reminds me each day that our kids are a provision, and that being a father is a core role in my life.

Friend to many: The Lord has called me to be a friend to many people.

It could seem from reading this that I have conquered all of my fears and the lies that kept me down. Yes and no. Yes, I now believe the truth about myself and not the lies, but I am still tempted, at times, to believe the lies. That is why praying this declaration each morning—reminding myself who I am—has become so important for me.

In reflecting about his own daily time with Jesus, one man I know said, "I come here each morning to remember who I am." That is what this prayer is all about, remembering the truth about who I am and what God the Father says about me. I wonder if that is why Jesus spent so much time alone with the Father.

What Did Jesus Believe about Himself?

On some level, Jesus had to believe what God the Father said about Him. But do you think He knew that as a baby—that He was God's chosen Son? Not likely. As a human, He had to grow into that awareness, like He grew into His awareness of everything else in the world.

There is a story in the Bible about Jesus going to the temple as a young boy. What did He believe about Himself that day? It's hard to know exactly. But we do see in this passage that He knew He still had much to learn: "Then, after three days they found Him in the temple, sitting in the midst of the teachers, both *listening* to them and *asking them questions*" (Luke 2:46, NASB). The assumption by some is that Jesus knew everything at this point in His life because He is God. I don't think that's the case.

Look at Jesus' next statement when His mother returned to retrieve him, "Why is it that you were looking for Me? Did you not know that I had to be in *My Father's house*?" (v. 49, NASB)

How did Jesus know it was His Father's house? Was He taught this from the very beginning, or did He know it because He *was* God? We get a clue in the next verse: "And Jesus kept *increasing in wisdom* and stature, and in favor with God and men" (Luke 2:52,

NASB). How can someone "increase in wisdom and stature" if he already knows fully? Jesus grew in His belief in the truth of His own identity, just like any other human.

According to the history, God the Father spoke directly to Jesus in a special way for the first time on the banks of the Jordan River. Jesus would have heard stories from His mother about who He was, and listened to many teachings, but there is no indication that the Father spoke directly to Him before He came out of the water. God said, "This is my Beloved Son, in whom I am well-pleased" (Matt. 3:17, NASB).

From that moment in the river, this voice was the primary voice Jesus listened to. Sure, He engaged in conversation with others and listened to the crowds and people in need, but all of these voices were secondary. The voice that really mattered to Him was the voice of the One who called him "Beloved." This was the voice that told Him the truth of who He was. Jesus listened to this voice all the time and embraced it as the most important truth in His life.

Apprehending the Truth

One might even say that Jesus *apprehended* the truth about what God the Father said about Him. Just like Jesus, you and I get to actively participate with God the Father in believing the truth about ourselves. You may remember that we looked at Ephesians 3:17 together in Chapter 2. Let's also look at the next verse, along with verse 17, to see the invitation to take hold of the truth for ourselves:

> *So that Christ might finally settle down and feel completely at home in your **innermost being** through your **belief in the truth** (that you are loved); and that you **having been** deeply*

*rooted and **having been** deeply and firmly founded in the supernatural love of the Father. (v.17)*

That you might have the power and be made thoroughly strong to apprehend . . . (Eph. 3:18a, emphasis added)

Two Greek words really shape the understanding of verse 18. The first is *exischyō,* pronounced "exis-hoow." We translate it in English as "may be able," however, this translation loses the emphasis on power and strength. Paul's prayer here is that we would be made *thoroughly strong.* How does that happen? What is he really praying?

Power and strength usually come from training, but in this case, Paul is continuing his thought from verse 17, about believing we are loved. The power and strength comes from an outside source (the source being Jesus) entering into those of us who dare to believe and agree we are loved.

Katalambanō (pronounced like it reads) is the big game changer in verse 18. We often translate it as "to comprehend," but comprehend doesn't completely work here because it carries the idea of mentally grasping something. A better word is "apprehend," since it suggests grabbing hold of something for oneself. The Greek word literally means "to take eagerly or to seize; to make something your own." Here lies the difference between understanding the love of God the Father as a concept (comprehend) versus actively participating (apprehend) with Him in allowing that love to finally sink in. Paul's overarching prayer in Ephesians 3:18 is that **we might apprehend the truth that we are loved.**

This word *katalambanō* speaks directly to me because I have known about the love of God for many years. I have written about it, sung songs about it, and spoken about it to others. But it was only after the exposure of lies and daily proclaiming of the truth about myself that the shift really took hold. I guess you could say I got apprehended, in a good way, and have continued to believe the truth about myself more each day.

My friend Blake, a police officer, has taught me a lot about the word "apprehend." He told me he's learned a great deal about the lies people believe from perpetrators he has arrested. One of the first things Blake would have them do was to write out their confessions. He would ask them to tell the truth about what they had done, because any process out of darkness involves truth telling. What Blake noticed, over and over again, was that when a person decides to start telling the truth about themselves, change can happen.

In fact, it happened for Blake personally in such a tangible way that, after moving up the ranks in his career, he found himself sitting across the desk from the head of the prominent law enforcement agency where he was employed. With a large file of cases from the past five years sitting on the desk in front of him, Blake's superior officer said, "How are you doing what you're doing?" And then his boss got really specific. "How did you get inside of this gang? How did the crime in this area drop 70 percent after you and your team left? How are you getting the results you're getting?"

Blake's first response was, "You don't want to know." But his superior pressed the issue, so Blake chose to answer the first question, about the gang member. "Sir, my wife and I invited this gang leader to our home for dinner. I told him his lifestyle was killing his neighborhood and that he was dying a slow death. I told him he could overcome fear, guilt, and shame through believing the truth about who he is: a son of God.

"I told him he could replace the lies he was believing with the truth about what God says about him. My new gang leader friend encountered Jesus that evening in our home and began to believe the truth about who he is. Not only did he change, but the gang he led—and the whole neighborhood—changed significantly for the better."

Blake's boss responded, "You are right, I don't like your answer, but I can't argue with the results you are getting. We are sending you to rougher areas where we can't seem to make progress right now. That is your new assignment." Blake and his family were sent to places no one could imagine would ever experience change. Yet, through inviting people to tell the truth about what they thought about themselves, exposing lies, and replacing those lies with the truth of what God thinks about them, they saw amazing changes happen in significant ways!

Apprehending the truth—laying hold of it for ourselves—and then replacing the lies we've believed about ourselves with God's truth is a key component of believing that we are loved. We, too, can hear the voice of the One who calls us Beloved. God the Father says the same thing about you and me that He says about Jesus. We are His beloved children. It's true. Isn't it time to start living like it?

✦ Belief On-Ramp #4 ✦

In this exercise, revisit the lies you realize you have believed about yourself. For some, this may mean you are recognizing for the first time that those voices in your head telling you that you are less than, not enough, imperfect, unworthy, etc., are not true, and are in fact, flat-out lies! Whatever those lies are, identify them and jot them down.

In addition, write down specific negative words or phrases that come to mind about yourself (such as for me, things like "I am a boy, not a man"). Then write down the opposite of those words. That is often where the truth is revealed about who we really are!

energetic amazed happy excited proud content
long determined eager loving motivated peaceful
gracious daring courageous assertive warm confident
hopeful comfortable receptive joyful calm forgiving
inspired grateful caring
in awe thankful

You might also find it helpful to read through my wife Anna's "Personal Declaration." Anna is artistic and creative, while I tend to be more structured and pragmatic. The ways we have pursued healing and our journeys toward believing we are loved have often looked quite different.

After a decade of feeling alone, distant from God, and negatively impacted by the lies of unworthiness, Anna has been actively pursing wholeness and healing in her life for the past eight years. She has done this through learning to hear the voice of Jesus, receiving counseling/emotional healing, deep friendships, and spiritual direction.

Here is her declaration, written using the template I suggest in this chapter. I share it with her permission:

God, You are my comforter, my living hope, and I claim victory and freedom today in the name of Jesus. You are powerful and loving, my daily hope and salvation, the author of my story.

I, Anna Petree, claim my identity as Your beloved daughter. Thank You for Your constant care of me and our family. You are a good and faithful Father. I know that I am unconditionally loved and completely forgiven for all the times I've chosen my own way instead of Your best for me.

Satan, you have no power over me! I renounce all fear and shame, claiming God's love, mercy and healing power over my body, mind, and spirit in the name of Jesus!

Today I choose to believe that my face and body are beautiful and perfectly designed by You, God. That I am "fearfully

BELIEVING THE TRUTH ABOUT OURSELVES

and wonderfully made." You know me intricately, and have a wonderful plan for my life. You are my refuge and strength, my hope, a very present help in times of trouble.

Father, I know that as I surrender everything into Your hands, You are trustworthy. You direct my steps and have my best interest in mind. I believe in Your awesome power to restore and heal any part of me that You desire.

May my life today be a reflection of Your love, grace, mercy, and hope as I seek to love myself, my husband, our children, friends, and neighbors today. You, Father, are the primary focus of my affection. I believe today that I am enough, that I am worthy of love and belonging.

I am a courageous warrior. I will not succumb to fear or despair! Thank you, Father, that Your mercies are new every morning. You are by my side every step of this day. I am Yours.

Now, write your own Personal Daily Prayer. It's perfectly fine if it is a rough draft; you can continue to tweak it over the upcoming weeks and months.

Personal Daily Prayer

My name is _____, Beloved, I am loved.
I am Your chosen son/daughter. I am family.
Your Spirit is in me. Jesus is formed and is forming in
me. I am an heir of Your Kingdom,
a prince(ess), a saint. I choose joy today!
I am a _____,

_____, _____,

_____, _____,

_____

_____

_____

_____

_____

_____

_____

(These words are examples of words that could describe the true you. Think, too, of the negative words that come to mind about yourself and write the opposite on these lines.) When you finish this exercise, read your prayer each morning when you awake. Try it for 30 days and see what happens.

Chapter Five

Understanding the Humanness of Jesus

Is the Jesus you've heard about a "Superman" Jesus?

If you have been a Jesus follower for any length of time, you've probably read some (or all) of the first four books of the New Testament, or "the Gospels." They're all about Jesus, and reading them is a great way to get to know Him better.

What do you think of Him when you read those stories? Does Jesus seem human or super-human? In other words, in any given situation, did Jesus respond as a human would, or as if He were God?

What you read in these next few pages may challenge your understanding of God, specifically Jesus. However, it may be helpful to know that nothing I am writing about is a novel, original thought. It is, in fact, an understanding of Jesus that dates back 2000 years. Let's dive into it . . .

Just How Human Was Jesus?

The apostle Paul's letter to the Philippians tells us, ". . . But (Jesus) emptied Himself, taking the form of a bondservant, and became as human beings are" (Phil. 2:7, Phillips). A lot of people have argued about what Jesus emptied Himself of, exactly. Most Christian scholars agree that when Jesus came to Earth as a human, He emptied Himself, or set aside, His divine attributes—that is, His omniscience (knowing everything), His omnipresence (being everywhere, always present), and His omnipotence (limitless in His power). As a human, He was limited in all these qualities simply because He had a human body. But let's set that thought aside for now.

My question is this: what if He didn't just *empty* Himself, but also *added* something? What if that something was human nature? If that were the case, then of course Jesus would have had to limit the access He had to His divine nature. He couldn't fully operate out of His divine nature *and* still have the full experience of being human. Those two natures contradict one another.

This is the really challenging part. How human was Jesus, really? He was born of human flesh, grew physically like any other human would, had veins of actual blood, got hungry, thirsty, and tired. He died a physical death. He felt human emotions including anger, despair, joy, grief, sadness, excitement, and wonder. Jesus struggled—He was tempted, confused at times, limited by others' lack of response, frustrated, and often lonely. It all sounds pretty human to me.

If I were Jesus and had a "God card" I could access anytime I wanted, I would have certainly used it to avoid the daily struggles of being human. However, although Jesus possessed His divine nature throughout His life on Earth, He mysteriously gave up His access to this nature in order to fully possess humanness. Let that sink in for a moment. *God, through Jesus, became like us.* I don't know about you, but this makes Jesus—and in turn God the Father—much more relatable and "follow-able" than a super-human, superhero-like God.

To be open to the idea that we are loved is to respond to a God who chose to be human and vulnerable. As Dan Brunner said in a lecture at Soul Formation Academy, "A human Jesus is a broken Jesus who identifies with our brokenness." Jesus, in His human nature, completely identifies with us! He gets it—our joy, our sorrow, our loneliness, our longings. Jesus meets us in our humanity. He is, after all, the fullest expression and example of what it is to be human.

Practical Desires, Human Needs

Perhaps one of the most vulnerable, human aspects of Jesus is His birth. If you pause and really think about it, it's quite remarkable! God, the creator of everything, comes to Earth as a human being in the very same way every other human enters the world. In doing so, God (through Jesus) becomes susceptible to pain, disappointment, the need to learn and not just know, temptation, physical aches, and uncertainty. This act of humility put Jesus in a position that forced Him to rely on faith and belief, not His divinity, in order to do the things He did: healing the sick and blind, performing miracles, and setting free those who were being held in bondage by the devil.

With that in mind, let's look at one story of Jesus together and imagine Him being very human, acting out of belief that the Father would show up and carry out His will. Walking in faith—and not because He already knew what was going to happen.

John 2 (NASB)

On the third day there was a wedding in Cana of Galilee, and the mother of Jesus was there, and both Jesus and His disciples were invited to the wedding.

So here's the scene: we have Jesus coming into town, and where is one of the first places He goes when He arrives? A wedding. This man had just begun His mission to bring truth to the world, yet He takes time to go to a party. Sounds pretty human to me. The God I heard about growing up didn't smile, didn't laugh, and especially wasn't about having fun, and yet here we see Jesus, God in the flesh, going to a wedding celebration.

> *When the wine ran out, the mother of Jesus said to Him, "They have no wine." And Jesus said to her, "Woman, what does that have to do with us? My hour has not yet come."*

Jesus is at this wedding party, and the unthinkable happens—the wine runs out. Now, if you were any kind of host in ancient Jewish culture, the last thing you wanted to happen at a party was for the wine to run out. Wine was a significant part of the culture and represented the celebration of friends and family. It wasn't generally a twisted and misused drug that people used to look cool, cope with life, or get drunk. Wine was simply the sign of a life enjoyed. Imagine being the host, knowing it was your responsibility to make sure the bride and groom were honored and people were having a good time, and you run out of the most important item at the party. So what happens? Jesus' mother suggests that Jesus do something about the problem, and His first response seems to be no.

> *Now there were six stone water pots set there for the Jewish custom of purification, containing twenty or thirty gallons each. Jesus said to them, "Fill the water pots with water." So they filled them up to the brim. And He said to them, "Draw some out now and take it to the headwaiter." So they took it to him. When the headwaiter tasted the water which had become wine, and did not know where it came from (but the servants who had drawn the water knew), the headwaiter called the bridegroom, and said to him, "Every man serves the good wine first, and when the people have drunk freely, then he serves the poorer wine; but you have kept the good wine until now."*

Next, Jesus does a very human thing. He appears to change His mind! He tells the servants to grab the six stone water jars in the corner, fill them with water, and bring them to Him. Then, He tells one of the servants to draw a glass of the water—which has now become wine—and take it to the master of ceremonies. As it turns out, the "new" wine is even better than the good stuff they had before, and with that, we have Jesus' first recorded miracle.

Jesus met a very human desire by providing additional wine for the wedding celebration, and through this miracle He cared for people in a unique way. I believe He performed this miracle out of faith in the moment, and not out of some pre-planned deal He conjured up with God the Father.

When Jesus gave instructions to the servants to fill the water jars, it is very possible He truly had no idea what the results would be. I believe, along with many other followers of Jesus throughout the ages, that in this miracle story (and in the many that would follow) Jesus was operating out of belief. I believe Jesus had learned to hear the voice of God the Father and, as He put it, chose to do what the Father told Him to say and do (John 8:28-29).

Jesus came to do for you and me what He did for the host of the party that day. He came to meet our most basic needs and desires, and to offer us real, authentic life. Being fully human and fully God, He has the ability to meet those needs and desires perfectly.

So if it's real life you are interested in, you're searching in the right place.

Embracing Jesus' Humanity

I remember exactly where I was sitting in the theater when I first saw the movie *Goodwill Hunting*. At that point in my life, I had just begun exploring the meaning of life and faith on a deeper level. I knew I had pain from my past, but had not yet set out toward healing.

Toward the end of the movie, the character Will Hunting has a final appointment with his counselor, Sean. This is what happens:

SEAN: "I don't know a lot, Will. But let me tell you one thing. All this history . . . (indicates file with pictures of abuse in his past). Look here, son. This is not your fault."

WILL: (nonchalantly) "Oh, I know."

SEAN: "It's not your fault."

WILL: (smiles) "I know."

SEAN: (he moves even closer) "It's not your fault."

WILL "I know."

SEAN: (moves even closer) "It's not your fault."

WILL: (dead serious) "I know."

SEAN: "It's not your fault."

WILL: "Don't f*&% with me. Not you, Sean."

SEAN: (moves even closer, almost face to face) "It's not your fault."

WILL: (tears start to flow) "I know."

SEAN: "It's not . . ."

WILL: (crying hard now) "I know, I know . . ."

Sean takes Will in his arms and holds him. Will sobs uncontrollably. After a moment, Will wraps his arms around Sean and holds him, even more tightly.

This scene from *Goodwill Hunting* is a picture of what it means to be human, open, vulnerable, and real. As I watched this scene unfold I had a lot of emotions swirling around inside of me—memories of my own pain, a longing for healing, and sheer marvel at the connection and empathy between these two characters. What I had just witnessed on screen was a human deeply identifying with another human in his pain, and both were impacted in a profound way.

Sean chose to enter into Will's pain, which is what totally changed the course for Will. Up to this point in the movie Will was relationally disengaged, fearful of vulnerability, and apparently feeling unworthy of love. It was empathy, deep empathy, from another human being (Sean) that changed Will's course in life.

Through His humanity, Jesus is offering us the same experience of empathy, only at a much more profound level. Because Jesus is fully human, He is able to enter into our pain and offer us the opportunity to believe that we are loved, just as we are today, in our present circumstances—which is what I caught a glimpse of when I watched the scene with Sean and Will in *Goodwill Hunting*.

If we fail to grasp and embrace Jesus' humanness, it's hard for us to realize how fully and deeply Jesus empathizes with us. The fact is that we can return to that scene, replace the characters, and grab hold of a better understanding of Jesus' humanity and what it means for us personally.

Understanding the fundamentally human nature of Jesus is a crucial step in the journey of believing the truth that we are loved. Through Jesus' full embrace of humanity, we have a Creator God who identifies with us. The very nature of God through Jesus is His humanity. Through Jesus, we have the fullest picture of what it means to be human, vulnerable, and real. We also have access to God the Father, just like Jesus did. It's up to us to seek out that line of communication and relational intimacy—and then to receive it.

Even Peter Had to Be Convinced

After His resurrection, Jesus asked Peter, "Do you love me?"* What Jesus was really asking was, "Peter, do you believe you are loved? Because if you do, you can't help but love me back."

---

*See John 21.

The English translation of this incredible scene fails us miserably. Peter's response was, "Yes Lord, you know that I love you." But that's not exactly what he said, when you look at it in the original language!

The first time, Jesus asked, "Peter, do you love me (*agapaō*) more than these (fish)?

Peter responded, "Lord, you know that I have an emotional fondness for you (*phileō*)."

Jesus asked again, "Peter, do you love me (*agapaō*)?" As Kenneth Wuest puts it in his expanded translation, Jesus was really asking, "Do you have a devotional love for me called out of your *heart* by my preciousness to you, a love that impels you to sacrifice yourself for me?"

Peter's response to this was, "Lord, you know I have a strong, friendly feeling (*phileō*) toward you." Do you see what's going on here? Peter wasn't directly answering Jesus' question, which means he actually *was* answering the question! And his answer was "No." At this point in his life, just after his denial of Jesus, Peter didn't believe he was loved, so how could he possibly respond with love? Emotional fondness, yes; friendliness, sure; but love, no way.

Until we believe at our core that we are loved, we cannot possibly love others. Peter couldn't do it and we can't do it, but there is hope! Jesus so deeply desires intimacy with us that He comes to our level, wherever we are today. Watch this.

In asking a third time, Jesus changed the question: "Peter, do you have a strong friendly feeling (*phileō*) toward me?"

And Peter responded, "You know that I have a strong friendly feeling (*phileō*) toward you." Wow! Jesus' desire was for Peter to know he was loved, that he was cared for even in spite of his denial, but Peter wasn't ready to fully believe he was loved. With His third asking of the question, Jesus seemed to be telling Peter it was okay he didn't fully believe he was loved that day. He accepted Peter where he was in the journey, with the hope that Peter would eventually believe it.

This tells me that regardless of where we are on the road to believing we are loved; the offer of Jesus is to meet us. But He also makes it clear that His foremost desire is for us to believe that we are His beloved, that we are loved.

Do you believe?

Answering the Question for Ourselves

In his talk "Moving from Solitude to Community to Ministry," Henry Nouwen said,

> *God has become so vulnerable, so little, so dependent in a manger and on a cross and is begging us, "Do you love me? Do you love me? Do you really love me?" That's where ministry starts, because your freedom is anchored in claiming your belovedness. That allows you to go into this world and touch people, heal them, speak with them, and make them aware that they are beloved, chosen, and blessed. When you discover your belovedness by God, you see the belovedness of other people and call that forth. It's an incredible mystery of God's love that the more you know how deeply you are loved, the more you will see how deeply your sisters and your brothers in the human family are loved."*

Let this sink in: as we consider the offer of intimacy—true, meaningful intimacy with Jesus—it changes the way we carry ourselves. All of the subconscious questions most of us ask when we enter a room are already answered: *Will I be accepted? Noticed? Does my presence here make any difference? Does anyone care that I am here? Will I be true to my conviction? Am I loved? Am I known? Am I understood?* All of these questions are already answered by the only One who has authority to truly answer them.

If we don't get these question(s) answered from God, nor come to believe in a deep place that we too are God's beloved, we will keep asking others to answer these questions for us. The only question worth asking is, "Am I loved?"—and the answer is unequivocally YES!

✦ Belief On-Ramp #5 ✦

Set aside time when you won't be interrupted. Watch the above scene from *Goodwill Hunting*, (available on YouTube). Imagine Jesus in that scene with you. Imagine Him saying something like this: "I can't be close to you physically right now, but I want to be. I want to physically sit next to you and look you in the eye from an uncomfortably close distance and wait until you look back at me. Then I have something to tell you. You are loved."

Jesus: "You are not alone. You are loved."

You: (nonchalantly) "Oh, I know."

Jesus: (moving closer) "You are not alone; You are loved."

You: (smiling) "I know. I've read John 3:16."

Jesus: (moving even closer) "You are not alone. You are so, so loved."

You: "I know; I sang 'Jesus Loves Me' growing up."

God the Father: "You are not alone; You are loved."

You: (dead serious) "I know."

Jesus: "You are not alone. You are loved."

You: "Don't f*&% with me, Jesus. This can't really be true."

Jesus: (coming even closer to your face) "You are not alone; you never have been. You are loved."

You: (tears start to flow) "I know."

Jesus: "You are not alone. You are loved."

You: (sobbing) "I know, I know."

Jesus: "Do you, really? Do you know that you are not alone, that you are loved? Not in your head, but in your heart, in your soul, in your innermost being?"

Spend some time meditating on this scenario. How does it make you feel? What thoughts come to mind? Do you have anything else you'd say to Jesus if He came and sat next to you and told you this? Use this time to journal and write down your answers to these questions, along with any thoughts or feelings that arise. What do you sense the Holy Spirit saying to you about them?

Chapter Six

Spending Time with God

I think it probably goes without saying that it's difficult to believe someone loves you if you don't have a relationship with them. And the easiest—and arguably best—way to grow a relationship with anyone is to spend time with them. The converse is also true: the less time you spend with someone, the more likely you are to drift apart.

For years I tried to avoid this reality when it came to my relationship with God. Quite frankly, I thought I was too busy, too tired, and too important to make time each day for God. I had to attend to the many needs of the day, and I did not have time to sit and be with the One who created me. I never even gave myself the opportunity to sit in God's presence and soak in His love for me. Prayer was perfunctory and often impersonal, and almost always list-driven. All that changed when I learned to spend time with, talk to, and really get to know my Heavenly Father.

What Does It Look Like To Pray?

When I was younger, I thought I knew what prayer was. Each night as I laid my head down on the pillow, I would list all of the people that were closest to me. I would ask the Lord to bless them and then I'd slowly drift off to sleep. I was careful not to miss a night because I was afraid of what would happen to these people if I didn't pray for them. I saw to it that they were protected by my prayers and believed that without me, these friends and family members would be in a rough place.

Over the years, my understanding of prayer has changed. While I still believe in the power of petitioning the Lord on behalf of family and friends, I have come to adopt a definition of prayer that I first learned from Henry Nouwen. *Prayer is being with God and God alone*. As I considered this definition of prayer, I had to honestly ask myself if there was space for that in my life. After all, this was Jesus' model of prayer and if I was seeking to pattern my life after Him, then I had to begin to create space in my life for God to get at me. If Jesus often spent time in solitude, I believe He is asking us to do the same.

I attended a seminar in 2000 where I was encouraged to spend daily time with Jesus. At that point in my life, spending time alone with God was sporadic at best so I decided to give it a try. The presenter of the seminar, Tom Raley, was 73 years old at the time, and he talked about how daily time in prayer had changed every aspect of his life. At one point Tom told us, "I started spending daily time with Jesus 42 years ago, and haven't missed a day." *WHAT!!! Was he serious?*

Before he ended the session, Tom gave us a loose framework for our own time with Jesus and challenged us to commit to thirty days in a row. I got home and decided to go for it. My journal entry that morning was "Day 1." After thirty days, I was in! (Like Tom, I committed to getting daily time with Jesus and haven't missed a day since.)

Here was Tom's framework: When you wake up in the morning say, "Good morning, Lord. Thanks for a good night's sleep. I look forward to being with you today." And then after that, to spend a few minutes doing each of these:

1. Praising
2. Giving thanks
3. Asking for guidance—reading Scripture and praying over your calendar for the day
4. Dedicating the day to the Lord
5. Interceding—praying for family and those you minister with and to
6. Petitioning
7. Meditating—picking out something from your time with the Lord that you can carry with you the rest of the day[3]

After a few years of using this model, I began to branch out to other tools. The devotional book *A Guide to Prayer for Ministers and Other Servants*[4] has been a great companion on this journey of learning to spend daily time with the Lord. This little book offers a daily Psalm, Scripture reading, and a reflection for the day. It is a great tool for someone starting out on a journey of daily time. For three years, I did the *One-Year Bible* (which provides a daily reading and it was fantastic). It got me deep into Scripture each day and provided grounding for my faith.

What I've learned from Tom and from my own experience over the past seventeen years is that a plan is very helpful. I don't mean it should be a formula, but without a plan, we often wander (and this is true of many other things other than prayer). To get up each morning and know how to begin my day with Jesus has been pivotal for engagement and longevity. I highly recommend it. Bottom line: if we are serious about making a relationship with God a priority, then following a plan that becomes a simple and flexible ritual can help lead to vibrant life in Jesus.

Learning to Listen

After a number of years of spending daily time alone with God in this way, I have realized that perhaps the most significant thing we can do in our time with Him is listen to His voice. You may be thinking, *What? Come on now, Shawn. How do you do that? What does that even mean?* I hear you. Developing the discipline of listening for God's voice did not come easily for me. In fact, in the early days I would get distracted by a thousand different things in one sitting. I was annoyed, impatient, and constantly looked at my watch to see when the pain was going to end. Yet slowly, over time, as I continued to return to this place of listening, I began to hear the voice of God.

Now, it wasn't an audible, booming voice that shot down from Heaven. Sometimes it was simply through Scripture, a passage in a book I was reading, or journaling. Other times it was through the still calmness that overcame me in the moment. But surely and incrementally, over the past 17 years of consistently showing up to listen, God has given me the ability to hear Him. He gives direction for my day, wisdom in decisions, discernment in the moment, and assurance that I am His son. And more than anything, His quiet whisper assures me that I am loved.

Dyan's Journey

I've known others who have shared a similar journey with God. One of those is my friend Dyan, who is an incredible woman. She loves life, is a people person, and is extremely passionate about caring for others. She and her husband Steve, along with their four kids, have been missionaries for 27 years, spending the past 15 years in Africa. In addition, Dyan founded Karama, an organization that helps alleviate poverty by restoring dignity through creative, purposeful work for artisans in Africa and beyond. Needless to say, Dyan could more than fill her days with worthy work that impacts others. However, she has chosen to begin her days listening to the truth about who she is.

For the past twenty years, Dyan has recited, memorized, researched, sung, journaled, painted, doodled, and prayed the identity that God has given her from the Bible. When she first started on this daily journey, Dyan admitted she had the hardest time believing in God's love for her personally. Of course, it was easy for her to see how He could love others. She knew He loved her in the "He made me so He 'has' to love me" sort of way, but Dyan did not see herself as beloved. She believed she was too unworthy.

Slowly, through a sprinkling of God's Word each morning, Dyan found verses that spoke of her identity in Christ. One by one, she began to collect these verses. For more than a year, she continued to add verses to a little slip of paper. Eventually, verses filled the front and back of the piece of paper, and Dyan couldn't believe how often the Bible spoke of how much God loved her!

During her time with God in the mornings, she began to recite these scriptures out loud. The list eventually got too long for her to read through each verse every morning, so she wrote all the verses in a journal and spent time meditating on one verse each day. Dyan now has 365 identity verses written down in a journal. She takes time each morning to sit with one of these verses and remind herself of the truth about who she is.

Dyan's morning rhythm begins with inviting the Holy Spirit into her mind, speech, and heart. She sits with God quietly, facing her hands downward to symbolize the things she wants to release and surrender that day (stress, worry, resentment toward another, etc.). Next, she turns her hands over, symbolizing her readiness to receive the truth that God has for her. It's a simple but meaningful practice inspired by a traditional prayer of the Quakers.

After she is prepared to receive, Dyan spends time with one of the true statements about her identity from Scripture. Sometimes she journals about how the verse is speaking to her that day, and other times she will meditate or draw. The important thing for her is to have her hands, heart, and mind open to believing the truth about herself. This incredibly simple discipline and routine helps Dyan fully receive and understand God's love for her, and opens up her heart to hear Him communicate with her.

Coming to KNOW

The next verse in the Ephesians 3 passage that we have been looking at together speaks to this growing reality in Dyan's life. (What follows may feel a bit academic, but stay with me; I believe it's helpful to understand this.)

So far we have looked at Paul's prayer recorded in Ephesians 3:16-18 (my own translation directly from the Greek text):

> *That He would make a covenant or grant to you, in proportion to His largeness and the wealth of His glory, **to be empowered** or made strong, with supernatural power through His Spirit **into** the interior or inside man . . . so that Christ might finally settle down and feel completely at home in your **inner self** through your **belief in the truth**; and that you **having been** deeply rooted and **having been** deeply and firmly founded in the supernatural love of the Father, That you might <u>have the power</u> and be made thoroughly strong to **apprehend** with all the saints, what is the width, and length, and height . . .*

Now consider the next verse, verse 19 (Greek understanding):

> *. . . and to understand with extraordinary knowledge the **supernatural love of Christ**, which goes way beyond head knowledge, that you might be filled unto all the fullness of God.*

"To know" in the English translation is the same as the word *ginōskō* in the Greek. *Ginōskō* speaks of knowledge that goes beyond the merely factual and into the realm of the experiential.

Today, we live in a fact-based society that worships knowledge. We live by the mantra "the more we know the more we can control." We like whatever is concrete and tangible. However, this verse communicates that Paul's prayerful desire was for the Ephesians to be *empowered* so as to **know the love of Christ that surpasses knowledge**. (Note this is not a petition that *the believers might love Christ more—as important as that is—but rather that they might understand* His love in an experiential dimension, that they would experience it first hand.

The "love of God" here cannot be adequately put into words, but it is the unconditional, sacrificial love which God is. Kenneth Wuest translates the last part of this verse ("that you may be filled up to the measure of all the fullness of God") wonderfully by saying, "Paul's prayer to the Father reaches its climax in this final, summarizing request. Thus we note that as believers are strengthened in the inner man through the Spirit and Christ dwells comfortably at home in their hearts through faith and they know in a personal, experiential way more of the immeasurable love of Christ, based on these spiritual dynamics, believers will be filled to the measure of all the fullness of God."[5]

So, the filling Paul talks about here at the end of verse 19 is the result of what he talked about in verse 17-19a becoming a reality in our innermost being, our inner self. This is not easy, and it takes time—a lot of time—but it's worth it. The fullness of God is power, and we are empowered, literally made powerful (in a good way), through experientially knowing that we are loved by God. There is nothing conceivable beyond the fullness of God; it is all the divine perfections of the Godhead as expressed in Jesus. This is the goal: to know that we are loved!

Being God's Beloved

I was first introduced to the term "beloved" through a cassette tape by Henry Nouwen titled "Moving from Solitude to Community to Ministry," which I mentioned earlier. I remember driving around in my pick-up truck 20 years ago, listening to the tape over and over. I still pull it out sometimes, track down a cassette player, and hear Nouwen's words again and again.

"Who am I? I am the beloved. That's the voice Jesus heard when he came out of the Jordan River: 'You are my beloved; on you my favor rests.' And Jesus says to you and to me that we are loved by the Father as he is loved." This sounded like a great concept many years ago as I drove around listening to that cassette tape. Noewen's message about being God's beloved slowly began to sink in as I made the commitment to sit with God each day.

In this journey of learning to believe I am loved, I have leaned more and more into solitude. I've learned to create space in my day to be with God alone. And quite honestly, it's changed my life. I like to think about it this way: each day has 1,440 minutes in it. Shouldn't the Creator of all things—the One who wants to spend time with me—get at least 20 to 60 minutes of my undivided attention each day? To me, the answer is quite obvious.

As I've continued to experience these quiet moments with Him over the years, I've learned that the commitment to spend time with God goes far beyond a time of silence. It's an invitation into intimacy. Real, authentic, all-encompassing intimacy. It's an invitation to become fully vulnerable, fully known, and fully exposed. Although I'm sure these words are scary for you to read (and for me to write!), this is the model of God.

✦ Belief On-Ramp #6 ✦

If you aren't currently in a rhythm of daily time with the Lord, I hope you'll give it a try. Set aside your first 10 minutes of the day (yes, before you grab your phone) and follow Tom Raley's loose model which I've repeated for you below. If you aren't a morning person, do this the last 10 minutes of your day. Try it for 30 days. If you miss a day, start over.

Here are some suggestions for your time with God:

1. Praise
2. Thanksgiving
3. Guidance—read Scripture and pray over your calendar for the day
4. Dedication—dedicate the day to the Lord
5. Intercession—pray for family and those you minister with and to
6. Petition—ask God to provide for your needs and concerns
7. Meditation—pick out something from your time with the Lord that you can ponder the rest of the day

Daily time with God and God alone changed Tom Raley's life. It changed mine, and my friend Dyan's, also. Your life, too, can be changed forever.

Chapter Seven

Taking a Day Away

My commitment to spend time with God each day has been transformational in my journey of believing the truth that I am loved. But it's only one of the many ways I've discovered to encounter and appreciate God's loving presence in my life.

Another tangible way I've learned more about the reality of God's love is through taking a day away from time to time. I'm not talking about a vacation, although that is vitally important to life as well. I'm talking about taking a whole day for *myself* to be with God. I know, it sounds a bit mysterious and maybe even downright weird. Most of us can't imagine taking even 15 minutes in a day to be silent before God and God alone, much less a whole day. What would we do with a whole day, unplugged, with just Him? You might be surprised . . .

Experiencing a Day Away

So, what could a day away with God look like? Before I get into the specifics of what mine have looked like, it might be helpful to get a glimpse into my friend William's journey with believing he is loved by God, and how taking time away with Him has been a powerful practice in William's life.

William has been an employee at a large corporation for over 15 years. He has made his way up the ranks over the years, experiencing not only career success but success in many other areas of life. A few years ago, William realized that there was a void, and he knew something was missing in his life. He began to explore faith in God and found a source of comfort that was new to him: spending time with His heavenly Father.

William is the kind of person who, when he discovers something he wants, he commits time and space to pursuing it. So, He began to practice daily "alone time" with God. Soon after that, he approached me and asked if there was anything else I could recommend to help him in his growing relationship with God. I suggested a day away—like I'm suggesting to you—and offered to go along with him, providing guidance along the way. He agreed.

William had a few things to do at the office in the morning, so I picked him up at work. We committed the late morning, afternoon, and evening to exploring this concept of a day away with God.

On the hour-long drive to our destination, William was honest about some of his thoughts in the days leading up to this time away. He told me he had almost cancelled several times, for a few reasons. The main reason was that "he just didn't have time for this." Another reason was that he was afraid of what might come up during an extended period of silence. And if something did come up, where would he find the time to deal with it afterward? The final reason was that his kids got sick. How could he take the time he could be using to help his wife with the kids and go off on his own? However, despite his reservations, William made the decision to take a risk and see what a day away with God might bring.

As we drove, the two of us talked about life in general—what was going well, what wasn't going well. He talked about his desire to grow deeper in his relationship with Jesus, and had questions about how to pursue that relationship while still meeting the many demands of work and family. In fact, we talked all the way to our destination, a small cabin overlooking the Puget Sound in northwest Washington State.

Upon our arrival, William and I began with 20 minutes of silent listening. Silence was a new experience for him, and although he felt distracted at times, he told me he was thankful for the opportunity to try something new in his journey with Jesus.

The most prominent feeling that came up for William in those 20 minutes (he told me later) was anxiety. It was mainly the overwhelming thought, "What do I do now that we are here? This feels vulnerable." Being a structured person, William was accustomed to working with an agenda and a list of desired outcomes. Without much structure to the time, William soon wondered if things were going to seem better or worse at the end of this day. Feelings of guilt for taking time off work and away from his family seeped into the first hour of our time away.

But William stayed in it. He began to journal about the fact that he had never set aside time like this to focus on God. After some time on our own, we came back together and read Matthew 5:

> You're blessed when you've worked up a good appetite for God. He's food and drink in the best meal you'll ever eat. You're blessed when you care. At the moment of being "care-full," you find yourselves cared for. You're blessed when you get your inside world—your mind and heart—put right. Then you can see God in the outside world. (vv. 6-8, MSG)

William commented that this was the first time he had ever read Scripture slowly and really taken time to ponder it. He used the word "consume" to describe his regular reading of God's Word. Verse 8 stood out to William, the idea that we are blessed when we get our inside world put right. He admitted he had spent many years getting his outside world put right, but had neglected the interior life. This was an opportunity to have time and space set aside to work on the inside.

Later that day, on the drive home, he told me it felt as if a literal and physical weight had been lifted off his shoulders. Prior to arriving to the cabin that morning, he hadn't even recognized there was a weight on him! As the busyness of life slowed down, he told me, hope kicked in. In fact, as the hours passed, William did not want to leave the cabin. Beyond the beautiful view and refreshing space we were in, he felt in his soul he was refreshed and in a place where God was meeting him in a deep way.

William has since returned alone for more days away with the Lord. He tells me he has noticed being away for a day not only provides an opportunity to be with God alone, but also a chance to consider his past and invite Jesus to heal his pain. Through these dedicated days with God, William has realized how much his past experiences affect him as an adult today. Having the space to access and mourn his wounds, losses, and regrets has allowed him to move forward in areas in which he previously felt stuck. He now finds himself looking forward to his extended times away, and says it has been a significant catalyst in his journey of believing that He is loved by God.

My Personal Day Away

The ways in which each of us will interact personally and intimately with God will differ, because we are all unique in our personalities, motivations, experiences, and needs. My experience was a bit different than William's, and yours will likely be different than mine. And that's okay. The great thing is that we can learn from one another and encourage one another in our experiences.

For me, somewhere during the process of learning to believe I am loved, I realized that my part was to respond to this supernatural love of Jesus with love of my own. I was a little surprised at this revelation because I thought I already had. After all, I had been getting up every day for years, literally, to get time with Jesus. I even talked about how He was first in my life. But as the layers of the onion peeled away, so to speak, and Christ settled down more deeply into my innermost being, my "heart" or *cardia* (Eph. 3:17), it became painfully clear that something was not quite right.

It had been a rough few weeks. Anna and I were seemingly on different planets. I was averaging four hours of sleep a night, and I sensed something was brewing. In my standard way of doing things, I tried to figure out how to fix what seemed broken. The encounter crescendoed with what became one of the more significant conversations I have had with my wife in our marriage. The pinnacle moment was when she said, "So, we are being completely honest?"

My response was, "We have to be if we are going to get to the other side of this."

She continued, "In 14 years of marriage I have never felt like enough. There is always something to work on, something to fix in our marriage, about me, about something we are doing or not doing. I rarely feel delighted in by you."

Whooohw! Not WOW but, *whooowh!* Those words were like a dagger to my heart and soul. I had worked tirelessly (or so I thought) over the course of our marriage to care for my wife. What had happened? How had my attempts come across so differently than I had intended?

Earlier that week I had listened to a podcast from Timothy Keller titled, "Spirituality and Christian Hope." It came back to me at that moment because his words explained exactly what had been going on in our home for years. In the podcast Keller asked the question, "Do you have in your mind the perfect picture of a relationship with your wife and kids? The perfect home? The perfect amount of money in your account? No sickness? Then you have the worst kind of idolatry!" Keller went on to make this statement, "If we don't love Jesus and get love from Him as our primary source, and make Him our main spouse, then we will never be satisfied and filled."

Thankfully, in the painful moment when my wife told me the hard truth through significant tears, the Holy Spirit took over and I was able to respond with compassion. Somehow there was not one defensive thought in my body. I moved a footstool in front of her chair, looked her in the eye, and began to say, "Anna, I'm sorry, I'm sorry . . ." over and over again. I then asked for her forgiveness and for the Lord's forgiveness for making his daughter feel the way I had for so many years.

Coming out of this significant time of clarity with Anna, I knew I needed to get away for a day of prayer to get direction on how to move forward in a healthy way. I borrowed a friend's cabin on Lake Roesiger, an hour from our home in Seattle. I didn't sleep well the night I arrived.

I sensed the Father had been preparing me for this time away in the days leading up to my trip. My Psalm reading for the week had been Psalm 27, "One thing I have asked from the Lord, that I shall seek: that I may dwell in the house of the Lord all the days of my life" (v. 4, Phillips). The day before I departed I was facilitating a men's group, the passage we read was Mark 8, "What good can it do a man to gain the whole world at the price of his own soul?" (Mark 8:36, Phillips)

Then, a C.S. Lewis reading I had come across the day after my conversation with Anna came to my mind, which stated, "The negative ideal of unselfishness carries with it the suggestion not primarily of securing good things for others (in my case, my wife), but of going without them ourselves, as if our abstinence and not their happiness was the important point."[6] Lastly, I recalled the counsel from my spiritual director from 20 years earlier, who had taught me that the goal of life is to become, "Passionately indifferent about all things except Jesus."

I had not done that with my wife. I had become passionate, overly passionate, about making sure everything was perfect, and that I was getting my needs met from this primary relationship.

As I awoke to the new day at the cabin on Lake Roesiger, I had my coffee and breakfast and anticipated the day in front of me. Something was calling me to the woods. Henry David Thoreau's words resonated deep in my soul: "I went to the woods because I wished to live deliberately, to front only the essential facts of life, and see if I could not learn what it had to teach, and not, when I came to die, discover that I had not lived.[7] Eagerly, I began packing my backpack and getting my clothes together, antsy to get out the door. And then I heard the whisper, echoing the message in Tim Keller's podcast, now coming to me as the words of Jesus to my heart. The words were, "Make Me your one true lover."

To be honest, I thought I had. Years of creating space for Jesus each morning, without missing a day—*surely that was enough, wasn't it?* But it wasn't. Somewhere along the way, many years earlier, I had gotten it in my head that having the perfect relationship with my wife Anna, the perfect family, the perfect home, enough money in the bank, and no sickness was the answer to life. If I could get all of that figured out, then I would be happy.

In my time with the Father that morning, even before I departed, He reminded me of Thomas Keating's definition of repentance: "Change the direction that you are looking in for happiness." I didn't realize fully until this moment that my primary source of happiness had become this unrealistic picture of life and marriage I had built in my head. So, on a foggy morning at the lake cabin, our dog Lucy and I headed out, backpack en tote and enough clothes to keep me warm and dry if it started raining.

After parking at the trailhead and securing my gear, I set out on a hike to a waterfall. The forest was quiet and serene. As I walked, one step after another, I reflected more about how far down this rabbit hole I had gone, and I began to get sick to my stomach. The more I pursued this dream of the perfect life and marriage, the less it seemed to be working out.

I found myself craving attention from my wife, spending more and more time trying to make her life easier, and more and more time trying to be the perfect dad for our kids. Anger, resentment, bitterness, and fear ran deep. I couldn't figure out what was happening. I was still getting my time in prayer each morning. I was doing everything I thought I should do—praying earnestly for Anna and serving her. However, in the process, I felt like I was losing my own soul. It was clear, I had made Anna the primary object of my attention instead of Jesus. As I took more steps I heard the voice again, the invitation, "Shawn, make Me your one true lover."

A stream is my favorite sound in the world. It's only fitting that the Father, who knows me more intimately than anyone, would invite me to this specific section in the woods. After hours of walking and pondering, I couldn't believe my eyes when I caught a glimpse of the waterfall through the trees. It was tall, loud, and very powerful. The beauty of the scene overwhelmed me.

Lucy and I hiked up the side of the stream until we made it to the base of the waterfall. I took off my backpack, threw my hands in the air, and yelled at the top of my lungs, "YES!!!" We had arrived. I didn't know what would happen next, but it seemed like the Lord was inviting me into something deeper. I sat down next to the base of the waterfall, and I simply listened.

Thirty minutes or so went by and I heard the whisper once again, "Shawn, make Me your one true lover." What happened next was not planned or scripted. In my experience, it was the kind of thing that can only happen when we give God time and space to do what He wants to do in our lives.

I got up from where I was sitting and looked for a large log that could serve as an altar. The log I wanted was in the middle of the river below the waterfall, but it was accessible. I retrieved it, then began to gather sticks, branches, and small pieces of wood to place on the altar. Next, I turned toward the waterfall and looked to the top to realize the power of water and be reminded of how it cleanses. As for the altar I built, I looked down at it and saw it as a symbol of all of the things I was turning to trying to get my deepest needs met.

The words echoed in my head one more time, *Make me your one true lover.* I spent some time there just sitting and simply being. Mentally, one by one, I relinquished each of the things on my makeshift altar to the Lord. After a while, I departed from the waterfall, gave one last look to the top as I rounded the trail, and went down to the stream below to let this new reality set in.

I'd had the foresight to throw a cigar into my backpack and I lit it and sat down. Lucy flopped down beside me in quiet companionship as I savored the moment (and the cigar) and reflected on the significance of the day. I remember thinking as I rested there underneath a tree with the stream in front of me, "I am lighter." Something shifted in me that day. It happened because I took the time to get away for a day, to unplug and allow Jesus to lead me deeper into relationship with Himself. What a gift!

✦ Belief On-Ramp #6 ✦

As you might imagine, this chapter's Belief On-Ramp is to plan a day away with God. I recommend at least six hours. In the chapter, I presented a suggested model, and you read about William's experience with a first day away. So now, go make it your own. Schedule it in your calendar. Unplug from the world and see what God has for you as you commit time and space to be with Him and Him alone.

As you do, here are a few questions to consider:

1. What (or who) is getting your primary attention?
2. What might you need to put on the "altar" in order to turn your primary affection toward Jesus?

A day away with God can take many different forms. The setting can vary widely. It can be outdoors, indoors, and can include multiple settings throughout the day. You could begin at a coffee shop, go for a hike, or have lunch at a restaurant off the beaten path. Think of a place you want to go, ideally a place that you can be alone in quiet for part of the day, and go there.

Here is a suggested structure for a "Day Away with God" (six-hour time frame):

Arrive and sit in silence for 20 minutes.

Read Psalm 27 slowly (read it four times with a two-minute pause between each reading).

Read John 15.

Write about two things that stood out to you from Psalm 27 and John 15.

Take 10 minutes of silence.

Spend 30 minutes reading a spiritual book.

Go for a walk or hike (at least an hour).

Eat a meal (or fasting for the day is a great option).

If you have a private spot, lay down for 20 or 30 minutes.

Repeat reading of Psalm 27 and John 15.

Write anything you are sensing from the Lord during this time away.

Take another 10 minutes of silence.

Do an additional reading from a spiritual book.
Take a 20-minute walk.
Write down anything you would like to incorporate into your daily
     schedule in the upcoming days.
Thank God for this time away.
Depart.

This is a simply a guide. Rest, real rest, is one of the best parts
of a day away with God. Relax and enjoy the day!

Chapter Eight

Doing "Nothing"

A few years after my commitment to spend time each morning with God, I found myself longing for even deeper connection with Him. But I didn't have the faintest clue where to start.

I remember pulling up to a morning meeting a few minutes early and doing a Google search on my phone: "intimacy with God." A book by Thomas Keating titled, you guessed it, *Intimacy with God*, popped up on my search. I ordered the book and awaited its arrival on our front porch. As I read the first few pages, I realized it was speaking to that very longing in my heart! I was being invited deeper into the journey of silence and solitude with God.

In the book, the author, Father Thomas Keating, describes a silent prayer practice that helped him (and me!) more closely experience God's presence. This method of prayer is both a relationship with God and a discipline to foster that relationship. It's called "centering prayer."

Now, if you think it's an arduous task to commit to occasionally spend a *day* away with God in a culture that screams out that you are as valuable as you are useful, try doing *nothing* for 20 minutes a day. It will either make you crazy or . . . you just might discover the secret that Jesus often leaned on: silence and solitude in the presence of the Father.

Embracing Solitude

I touched on solitude earlier but I want to circle back and go a little more in depth on it here. It's so counterintuitive to our culture; it really does take effort to learn to cultivate this spiritual discipline.

We can see in the Gospel accounts that time alone with God was very important to Jesus:

> *In the early morning, while it was still dark, Jesus got up, left the house, and went away to a secluded place, and was praying there. (Mark 1:35, NASB)*

> *So Jesus, perceiving that they were intending to come and take Him by force to make Him king, withdrew again to the mountain by Himself alone. (John 6:1,5, NASB)*

> *It was at this time that He went off to the mountain to pray, and He spent the whole night in prayer to God. (Luke 6:12, NASB)*

We don't know what happened between Jesus and the Father in these times of solitude, but we do know that quiet, reflective time with the Father was a priority to Jesus.

By the world's standards, some might have said Jesus was "wasting" time. Not being "productive." Not "accomplishing" anything. The truth is that Jesus was operating on a completely different value system, one that we are wise to consider if we, too, want to draw close to the Father.

The Psalmist David also experienced this, saying, "My heart has heard you say, 'Come and talk with me.' And my heart responds, 'Lord, I am coming'" (Psalm 27:8, NLT). In that place, he could open himself up to the Lord and commune deeply with Him. David wrote of this practice: "Search me, O God, and know my heart; test me and know my anxious thoughts. (Psalm 139:23, NLT). When we sit quietly in the presence of the Lord and invite

Him to search us, we join David and a long line of spiritual giants who have experienced this before us.

In times like these, we can receive the ministry of the Holy Spirit, whom Keating referred to as "the Divine Therapist." Jesus described this work of the Holy Spirit also, and I love how the Amplified Bible translates His words: "But the Helper (Comforter, Advocate, Intercessor—Counselor, Strengthener, Standby), the Holy Spirit, whom the Father will send in My name (in My place, to represent Me and act on My behalf), He will teach you all things. And He will help you remember everything that I have told you" (John 14:26, AMP).

The Work of the Divine Therapist

In these times of solitude, the Holy Spirit, our Counselor, our "Divine Therapist," may choose to delve deep into our life history layer by layer, throwing out the junk and preserving the values and impressions that were appropriate to each stage of our human development. According to Thomas Keating, in people who experience this, God's Spirit seemingly works backwards through the successive stages of their lives: old age (if that's where they are starting), mid-life, early adulthood, late adolescence, early adolescence, puberty, late childhood, early childhood, infancy, birth, and even pre-birth. Eventually the Spirit begins to dig into the bedrock of their earliest emotional life, where the feelings of rejection, insecurity, lack of affection, or actual physical trauma were first experienced.[8]

Does this prospect interest or intimidate you? Perhaps both. Many of us are afraid of being alone with our thoughts. Many have spent years suppressing, medicating, drowning, or escaping them. Being alone with God can seem an intensely vulnerable place— but it can also be intensely healing and strengthening.

I'm sure centering prayer is not the only way to practice reflective time alone with God, although it is one that has been immensely helpful and meaningful to me. If it interests you, I hope you will do your own investigative work into Thomas Keating's writings and prayer practices, beyond the brief synopsis I can share here.

Basically, what centering prayer looks like is a circular process consisting of four major "moments." The first moment is a sacred **word** (or it may simply be a breath) as the symbol of our consent to God's presence and action within us. This gently establishes our attitude of waiting on the Lord with attentiveness. The second moment is one of **rest**, which we could also refer to as peace, interior silence, contentment, a sense of coming home, of well-being, and most of all, God's presence.

The third moment in centering prayer is a kind of **unloading** of the unconscious. That's a good way to describe the sensation of the bombardment of thoughts and feelings that can surge into our awareness at this point, the "jumping monkeys," if you will. Sometimes it seems like these thoughts have no relationship to anything that's been going on in your life lately. It's not necessarily a bad thing, though. When our body, mind, and spirit are deeply resting in this way, our defense mechanisms relax. Oftentimes, the undigested emotional material of our early life emerges from our unconscious in the form of a "bombardment" of thoughts and primitive emotions that need to be purged.

Getting rid of this primitive emotional material is the fourth moment of the circle. For someone who has carried this emotional pain for twenty or thirty years (or longer), the **evacuation** part may feel painful. But if we're doing this on a daily basis, as I have come to do, we come to trust our Divine Therapist to help us sort it out.

A single period of centering prayer might take me through each of the "four moments," or none at all. The goal is not to complete the cycle, but to remain in a state of contemplation for fifteen to twenty minutes. The hope is that we will learn to trust God to lead us through intentional times of "doing nothing," exposing our inner selves freely to Him. My experience is that through persisting in this practice, the real issues assert themselves. As a result, a growing trust in God has enabled me to experience deep healing as well as a deeper sense of God's love and care.

Practicing Centering Prayer

For the first few years, I sat with a wheel diagram from Keating's book in front of me, illustrating the practice of centering prayer, and used this diagram as a guide to help me subconsciously flow through the four moments. Some of my prayer sessions would be amazing, almost indescribable, and some sessions would feel like I was walking through mud in boots two sizes too big. The diagram is now etched in my mind and I am able to simply close my eyes and allow myself to travel through the moments one by one. (I realize this might sound a bit whacky, possibly even a little too Zen, but my experience of "doing nothing" with God for 20 minutes a day has been so life giving that I am okay with the mystery of it.)

Most of my centering prayer times are not remarkable, in the sense of nothing earth-shattering or notable happens. Occasionally, though, a session can be quite profound.

One morning, I awoke and entered into my normal routine. Over the years, my *word* has changed a few times, and for the past few years the word has been "allow." Sitting in my chair, eyes closed, I begin to whisper my prayer word, not out loud, but internally, *allow*. Like most mornings, my mind began to wander, so I returned to the word. It wandered again, and again I returned to the word.

After a number of minutes passed, I felt myself entering into the second moment, *rest*. The remainder of the session I was only barely aware of, as I went into a sort of semi-conscious state. I sensed the Holy Spirit inviting me into the third moment, *unloading*, and I heard him say these words to me, "Shawn, you are forgiven and fully cleansed. You are healed of all lies, deceit, shame, and tendencies to hide."

During this time of mystery, I had the impression of Jesus taking me to the Father. God the Father grabbed my face in a gentle way and looked me right in the eyes, repeating the same thing I imagined Jesus saying to me, "Son, you are forgiven and fully cleansed. You are healed of all lies, deceit, shame, and tendencies to hide." As I completed the fourth moment, *evacuation*, I felt a sense of release and relief. I had been met by God in a special way that morning.

A New Experience

My friend Brian was the first (besides my wife) to notice a change in me after I began practicing centering prayer on a consistent basis. We were driving home from a weekend away with some other guys and he told me he had seen a new calmness in me that hadn't always been there. He commented that this shift coincided with me beginning my daily centering prayer rhythm. With that in mind, Brian asked if I would be up for meeting periodically to teach him what I had learned about this practice.

Brian is a Type-A MBA with three young kids, and an active church and community life. He spent his thirties trying to climb the corporate ladder, working lots of hours at a sexy, high-tech company while also trying to be a paragon of the "Christian" husband, father, and friend. It only took a minor career setback for him to realize that his hope and identity were, admittedly, sorely misplaced. Soon, Brian found himself in a depressed and lonely state.

Brian and I were spending a lot of time together during this season of life and I remember sitting with him when he said, "Shawn, I thought I believed that Jesus was my purpose, and the love of my life, but my response to this pain at work is revealing the truth. I have allowed a performance-based value system to slip into my DNA." It became clear to Brian that Jesus wanted to take him deeper. What had started as a mid-life crisis opened him to a new way of receiving God's love.

Brian and I began to meet regularly to go through Keating's book, *Intimacy With God*, and follow the model laid out in this chapter. Brian began the seemingly foolish practice of "doing nothing" for 20 minutes every single weekday, allowing the Holy Spirit to examine and bring God's healing into his inner world. He's told me he doesn't believe he would have discovered this deeper love of God without the pain of personal failure—and his commitment to learn the value of sitting with God and God alone. He says now, "If you struggle to believe God loves you when you are sweating to make it all happen, perhaps it's time to embrace the sweetness of doing nothing, on purpose, with The Beloved."

Perhaps it is . . .

✦ Belief On-Ramp #7 ✦

The objective in centering prayer is not to push thoughts away, but instead to express your intention to love God in order to be in His presence, submitting to the healing activity of the Holy Spirit.

A typical centering prayer session is twenty minutes in length. It starts with choosing a "prayer word" and then calmly, peacefully, and lovingly repeating it silently—i.e., "saying" it in your mind, and not speaking it out with your lips.

Find a quiet, comfortable place to do this, one you can return to regularly. My ideal spot to spend time with the Father is next to a stream, or in my living room if I can't be outdoors. With my eyes closed, I can imagine my special spot by the stream. If a distraction arises (the jumping monkeys), simply acknowledge your mind's wandering, send your distracting thought downstream, and return to focusing on your prayer word. You can do this as many times as necessary throughout the course of your prayer time.

I encourage you to give it a try. Here's how:

1. Sit comfortably in a quiet place where you are not liable to be interrupted. Place your feet flat on the floor and keep your hands loosely folded in your lap or flat on your knees. It is better to use a chair with a moderately soft covering and without close fitting arms. Your eyes should be closed and your head held at a comfortable angle. (If you have an illness or physical disability, sit or lie in whatever way that suits your condition.)
2. If I were to ask you, "Where is the place that you feel most peaceful and close to God?" what would your answer be? For me, my spot is in my camping chair next to a stream in the San Juan Islands. Perhaps for you it is a place in the mountains among the trees, overlooking a beautiful vista, or by the ocean listening to the lapping of the waves on the beach at sunrise. Can you envision the place that is unique to you in your mind? It can be helpful to close your eyes and imagine your special spot with a seat saved for you as you join the Holy Trinity, who are together inviting you into conversation with Father, Jesus, and Holy Spirit.
3. Take a moment to relax. It is helpful to take three deep breaths. Fill your lungs by expanding your stomach. Hold the breath for about five seconds and then slowly exhale. Do this three times. I usually do this with a very brief prayer to each person of the

Trinity. First breath: "In the name of the Father"; second: "In the name of the Son"; third: "In the name of the Holy Spirit."

4. Say a brief prayer in your own words expressing your love for God and your desire to spend these few moments embracing Him in your love. It can be something like this:

> *Dear Father in Heaven, I love You. I want to love You more. I know that You love me and You have given me the grace to want to spend these twenty minutes in Your presence. I have chosen the prayer word, "Abba," Father (or whatever word you have chosen), to express this love I have for You. In the power of Your Holy Spirit and united to Your son, Jesus Christ, I now offer You my love through this prayer.*

5. Next, calmly, peacefully, and lovingly listen with the ears of your heart to your prayer word as you allow it silently to repeat itself. Do not whisper it out loud or even use your tongue or lips. Recognize that by this word you are expressing your love for God. Continue to do this fifteen or twenty minutes or longer if you feel called to do so.

6. Whenever distracting thoughts come (those dang monkeys again) and you find you have given in to them and allowed your prayer word to stop, simply send that distracting thought "downstream" and say: "I will go back to my prayer word," and do so. Do this as often as is necessary—even many, many times during a twenty-minute meditation.

7. If, during your prayer time, you should fall asleep, just thank God for the blessing of sleep and go back to your prayer word. Do not be concerned about this—God is not!

8. Sometimes you will "transcend" your prayer word. That is, as you are silently loving God in the chamber of your heart, your prayer word may stop and you will be in silent repose, loving

God without words and without symbols. This is fine. When you realize that you have done this, just say: "I will go back to my prayer," and do so. Time will pass very quickly when this happens.

9. When you think your time is up, look at your watch. If you still have a few minutes, go back to your prayer until twenty minutes is up. Then very slowly begin to pray aloud as you would like for a couple of minutes—perhaps something like the Lord's Prayer, a Psalm, or another prayer of your choosing—so that it takes you a full two minutes to say it. If you find that you would like to go back to your loving prayer, and you have the time, do so. Otherwise your centering prayer time is finished.

Chapter Nine

Reading the Gospels

My experience of "doing nothing" for 20 minutes each morning has been powerful, and an important part of my journey in believing the truth about myself.

Another helpful practice has been reading the Gospels for depth and not for distance. Now, you might be wondering at this point, what time does this guy get out of bed to do all this!? Keep in mind that the point is to connect with God. Over time, I have adopted different rhythms and have figured out creative ways to incorporate these rhythms into my day. (So I don't have to get up as early as you might think!)

In this chapter I will be introducing you to a practice that has been particularly encouraging for Anna and me. We pick one of the four Gospels (Matthew, Mark, Luke, or John) and go through the entire book slowly, story by story, using an ancient method called *Lectio Divina* to guide our time of reading and listening.

This ancient method has been kept alive throughout the centuries in the monastic tradition, and, in recent years, many people in a variety of faith traditions have discovered and come to treasure it. Practiced at one time by most followers of Jesus, *Lectio Divina*, Latin for "sacred reading," is a slow, contemplative praying of the

Scriptures that enables a person to experience a sense of union with God through His Word, the Bible.

Like Brian, whose story I told in Chapter 7, most of us have a tendency to "consume" what we're reading, which is kind of like eating so fast you hardly taste your food! *Lectio Divina* helps us slow down, savor, and digest the scriptures we're reading. It focuses on loving God and being loved by God through His Word.

The practice begins by choosing a brief text of Scripture. It makes no difference which text it is, as long as there is not a set goal of "covering" a certain amount of text. In other words, it is not important how far you read, but how deeply you are able to consider the words. In sacred reading, it is necessary to remain with the words long enough to discover some of the mysteries that are hidden there. One of the mysteries for me is how much emphasis is placed on belief in many of the Gospel stories.

Discovering Belief in the Stories of Jesus

A few years ago, I read the story of Lazarus over a period of a few days. It's too long of a story to do in one *Lectio* sitting, so I broke it up into three readings. What I discovered is that it is one of the most emphatic stories of belief in the Gospels!

The scene: Jesus' good friend Lazarus has died and Lazarus' two sisters send for Jesus. Lazarus must have thought he was pretty good friends with Jesus. Even though he was sick, he had seen and heard all that Jesus was doing. I'm guessing he had hope that he would be healed, just as Jesus had healed many others. But lying on his deathbed, breathing what seemed to be his last, Lazarus' opinion of Jesus might have changed. His friend did not appear at the eleventh hour as he and his sisters hoped.

There is so much talk of belief in this story that the only proper recap is to just quote the text in John 11:

So Jesus then said to them plainly, "Lazarus is dead, and I am glad for your sakes that I was not there, so that you may believe; but let us go to him."

Martha then said to Jesus, "Lord, if You had been here, my brother would not have died. Even now I know that whatever You ask of God, God will give You."

Jesus said to her, I am the resurrection and the life; he who believes in Me will live even if he dies, and everyone who lives and believes in Me will never die. Do you believe this?"

Jesus said to her, "Did I not say to you that if you believe, you will see the glory of God?" So they removed the stone. Then Jesus raised His eyes, and said, "Father, I thank You that You have heard Me. I knew that You always hear Me; but because of the people standing around I said it, so that they may believe that You sent Me." When He had said these things, He cried out with a loud voice, "Lazarus, come forth."

Therefore many of the Jews who came to Mary, and saw what He had done, believed in Him. (John 11:14-15, 21-22, 25-26, 40-43, 45, NASB)

This encounter with Lazarus is a pivotal moment in the Gospel story. Jesus tells the disciples from the onset that this experience with Lazarus is all about belief. Think about it. Jesus went to incredible lengths here to get people's attention. These were friends Jesus loved. Mary, Martha, and Lazarus were in the "inner circle," yet Jesus allowed Lazarus to die anyway.

I had read this story in John many times, but somehow I missed it that the plot to kill Jesus was primarily about belief. Here's what I mean. As a result of Jesus raising Lazarus from the dead, we get this outcome: "Therefore many of the Jews who came to Mary, and saw what He had done, believed in Him. But some of them went to the Pharisees and told them the things which Jesus had done." (John 11:45-46, NASB).

Once the Pharisees heard the story about Lazarus and about the number of people beginning to believe, they formed a council. This is the part I never paid attention to. A committee was formed to deal with the very issue of belief!

Once the committee got together, they begin to feed off one other. I am sure each had stories about Jesus they had either witnessed first hand, or that someone had told them. They probably began with a few instances and then the group mentality took over and the stories were flowing. John gives a crescendo summation of the council meeting: "If we let Him *go on* like this, all men will believe in Him, and the Romans will come and take away both our place and our nation" (v.48).

The council was scared. They didn't want to give up their way of life. Even though they were under Roman rule, they had figured out how to work the system. Too many people believing in Jesus would mess up their way of life, and they weren't going to allow that to happen. At the end of this story John tells us, ". . . from that day on they planned together to kill Him" (v.53). The people's growing belief in Jesus was the catalyst that led to His death.

My favorite part about this miraculous day with Lazarus is Martha's response to Jesus: "But I know that even now God will give you whatever you ask." Faith, belief! In spite of what seemed hopeless, Martha believed.

Jesus' next statement of belief is both for that moment and a foreshadowing of what will become the reality for all who believe. Jesus promises them eternal life, and He doesn't stop there! He follows that remarkable assurance with, "You will see the glory of God." Astounding! No wonder many of the people put their faith in Jesus that day after He raised Lazarus from the dead. It strengthens my commitment to do the same.

Believing God Speaks through Scripture

As I mentioned, Anna and I regularly practice *Lectio Divina* reading together. We throw on our tennis shoes, leash up the dog, hit the trail close to our house, and read and meditate on Scripture as we walk and talk.

Years ago we came across this statement of Jesus that stopped us in our tracks (literally!): "I promise you," returned Jesus, "nobody leaves home or brothers or sisters or mother or father or children or property for my sake and the Gospel's without getting back a hundred times over, now in this present life, homes and brothers and sisters, mothers and children and land—though not without persecution—and in the next world eternal life." (Mark 10:28-30, Phillips). At the time, we believed God was speaking to us directly through His Word about His provision for a house. We held fast to this promise and prayed over it diligently. It was amazing to see God's answer unfold!

When she and I met, Anna and I knew early on that we were called to a lifestyle of ministry. We weren't sure how it would play out, but ministry would be our lifelong call. The only problem is that a ministry lifestyle is not necessarily conducive to owning a house. I am not talking about a home; Anna is crazy gifted at making a house into a home. I mean owning a house and, for us, part of that challenge involves having a home big enough for hospitality. She and I both love to host people and like to have a large enough place for people to gather.

After our first two years of marriage, Anna and I moved from West Texas to Washington State. Let's just say I had major sticker shock when we got to town. After realizing that houses were out of our price range, we started looking for an apartment. In the meantime, we were living with a couple who "happened" to be realtors. Before we knew it, they had found a wonderful house for us that fit our desires perfectly! We qualified for a loan (this was before the days of banks handing out money for home loans) and the financial side of things worked out well. We were thrilled!

A few years later, we were working on starting a family and hoped we could get a home our family could grow into. We remembered the promise God had given us years earlier, from Scripture, and we continued to believe.

Some friends of ours had a Christmas party that year and announced at the end of the party that they were going to be selling their home off market. This home was way out of our league! The wife was a professional interior designer and practically every square inch of the home had been remodeled. I remember getting into the car after the party and Anna commenting to me that she wished there was some way we could buy that home. It was perfect for a young family and had an amazing great room for entertaining and hosting gatherings.

Two months after the party, I was on the golf course with my friend who owned the house and he told me the price he would be willing to sell the house for. To us! I was floored! After running numbers the previous two months, I knew we would be able to pull it off. Anna was blown away when I got home that day. We thanked the Lord again for His promise, and for providing for us in abundance.

Five years after moving into that dream home, we sensed that our ministry was shifting to Seattle. That's all well and good, but we are talking about moving to Seattle in 2010! No banks were loaning money and even if they were, the Seattle market was out of our price range. About the same time we were praying about a move to Seattle, my new ministry partner got a call that his name was up on the waitlist for a retirement community he and his wife were hoping to go to in the next one or two years.

Even though their name came up early, they decided to go ahead and move.

I asked Connie (my friend) about his house. He told me he had sold the house a few years earlier to a company that had bought a whole row of houses for their employees, and that he and his wife had been renting back from that company. He said he would be happy to call and inquire on our behalf, but to his knowledge only employees of this company were offered the opportunity to lease these homes once the original owner moved out. After six weeks of waiting, we heard back from the company: they made an exception and we were offered the home!

The only problem was that, in the excitement, I didn't fully consider the monthly lease cost. After talking with Anna, I realized the home was 500 dollars a month more than we could afford. I called the leasing agency and explained my dilemma. I asked if any of the other homes on the street were available. The agent responded with, "Let me ask the owners and we'll just see." Later on that day, I got an email that the company was willing to lower the rent by 500 dollars a month! We were stunned and once again, amazed at the Lord's overwhelming provision.

The story with the house in Seattle didn't end there. Remember Tom Raley, whom I wrote about in Chapter 6? The man who encouraged me to start spending daily time with Jesus? Before we moved into the house, I talked with Connie about the history of his home. He and his wife had lived there for 40 years, and—wonder of wonders—had purchased that house from Tom and Reece Raley! As I did the math, I realized that Tom Raley began his daily time with Jesus in the same house in which I now spend my daily time with Jesus. Are you kidding me?!

I smile every time I think about it. It's a great reminder that the Lord goes way before us, and many times He will use Gospel truth to remind us of His promises and provide a catalyst for us to believe.

A Charge to Believe: Christ in YOU!

My friend and mentor, the founder of Teleios, practiced reading the Scriptures for depth and not for distance for many years. In 2010, he was diagnosed with pancreatic cancer. There is no known cure for this type of disease. In a few short months, Connie went from fully well to counting the weeks left of his life on Earth.

At what would become his final Teleios board meeting in December, Connie gave the devotional. That morning Connie spoke passionately from one of his favorite passages that he had read often and deeply over the years, Colossians 1:15-29 (NASB). His reflections have huge implications about how we go about our lives in belief:

v.15 ("He is the image of the invisible God, the firstborn of all creation.")—Jesus is our God, our Savior, the one who has come for us.

v.20-23—We have all been reconciled! The problem is we don't recognize that this has happened. (Don't forget that we are the Gentiles, the "outsiders.")

v.24—We are to rejoice in our sufferings. (We had the privilege of watching Connie rejoice to the very end. Two days before he passed, he said, through broken words and with a lot of pain, "Whatever you are doing with me, Lord, may Your name be lifted up.")

v. 26-27—The mystery is Christ in you! We have the mind of Christ; the enemy tries to take this reality from us.

v. 28-29—These are our marching orders: "We proclaim Him, admonishing every man and teaching every man with all wisdom, so that we may present every man complete (*teleios*) in

Christ. For this purpose also I labor, striving according to His power, which mightily works within me."

Each of these above reflections is directly from Connie. This was his final summation that morning:

> *Our presence in this world is powerful because God is in us! Just by building friendships and relationships, not even by speaking the name of Jesus, we are carrying out the work of Christ. Salvation is our opportunity to live life on Earth as Christ lived. "Now this is eternal life: that they know you, the only true God, and Jesus Christ, whom you have sent" (John 17:3). Eternal life begins today, men. Know God and continue to build friendships with others. As you do that the whole world will be changed.*

Connie taught everyone around him (me included) to make the truth of the Gospels, truth about the person of Jesus, the foundation of our life and how we relate to God and to people around us. It is foundational for our belief about God, and believing how He wants to speak to us and work in our lives.

If we've been around church and the Bible any length of time, it's easy for these much-read, much-loved passages of Scripture to become overly familiar. That was certainly the case for me, which is why *Lectio Divina* was such a gift—it helped me to experience the passages in fresh, revitalizing ways. I hope you'll give it a try.

✦ Belief On-Ramp #8 ✦

Pick a Gospel story and take 20 minutes or so to approach it using the *Lectio Divina* model I describe above. To begin this practice, sit in a comfortable position that will allow you to remain alert and let yourself be quiet for a few moments. Or, if you prefer, go on a "*lectio* walk" with God, like Anna and I like to do.

Next, read from the Gospel story you've chosen, reading slowly and carefully, and continue to read until you sense a prompting to stop. Savor each portion of the reading constantly, listening for the "still, small voice" of Lord—an impression of a word or phrase that the Holy Spirit appears to be highlighting to you that day. Don't expect lightning to strike or an overwhelming feeling of transcendence. In *Lectio*, God is teaching us to listen to Himself, to seek Him in silence. God does not reach out and grab us; but rather softly, gently invites us to know that He is present with us.

Next, pause for a few minutes and read the same verses again aloud, listening again for a word or phrase that is speaking to you in the moment. Memorize it and slowly repeat it to yourself, allowing it to interact with your world of concerns, memories, and ideas. Don't be afraid of what might feel like random thoughts; they are not necessarily distractions. Memories or thoughts are simply parts of yourself which, when they rise out of thoughtful prayer, are asking to be given to God along with the rest of your inner self. Allow this pondering to lead you into dialogue with God.

Next, read the same passage slowly for a third time and, when you have finished the reading, speak to God. This is also a great opportunity to "speak" to Him through journaling your thoughts. You can do this in writing or, if you prefer, using your computer or tablet—however you find you can most comfortably and efficiently express yourself.

For example, if you notice yourself being stoic and holding back from allowing yourself to feel in a certain relationship or situation, then you might say something like, "Lord, I'm doing it again. I notice myself self-protecting and not allowing myself to fully feel the pain of the situation I am in. Would You please give me the grace to feel fully and love deeply? I know that ability only comes from You."

Or, like Anna and I experienced in the story I shared in this chapter, you may sense the Lord speaking to you about a promise He has for you, or a word of encouragement. Maybe there is a gentle word of reminder or correction. Interact with God as you would with someone who knows, loves, and freely accepts you. Offer to Him what you have discovered in yourself during your experience of reflection.

Finally, read the passage one final time and simply rest quietly in the presence of God. When you sense the Holy Spirit inviting you to return to your pondering of the Word or to your conversation with God, do so. Learn to use words when words are helpful, and to let go of words when they are not necessary. Celebrate the truth that God is with you in both words and silence, in spiritual activity and inner receptivity.

Chapter Ten

Persevering in Belief

Anna and I are both from big families. Each of us grew up in a home with four siblings, so our natural desire was for a big family of our own. In our early thirties, we began to talk about kids and the timing of trying to get pregnant. We had our timeline and God had His (that's usually how it works in most instances, right?).

During our first two years of trying to have children, we held it loosely, as we both were enjoying our careers and had a full plate. But starting in year three, we began to get uneasy and wondered if having a family would be in our future. We did all of the testing and things seemed to be working the way they were supposed to, but at the end of year three we still found ourselves "without child."

About that time I read Psalm 127, which says, "Children born to a young man are like arrows in a warrior's hands. How joyful is the man whose quiver is full of them!" (Psalm 127:4-5a, NLT). I was bordering on no longer being a "young man" and wondered if this promise of God included me (us). By this time, getting pregnant was consuming our thoughts. We cried out to God, begging him to provide a child for us. It was then, after much prayer and anguish, we were overjoyed to find out that Anna was pregnant, three and half years into our journey of trying to conceive.

Despite the incredible encouragement I have received from my growing awareness of how much God loves me, my journey of belief the past ten years has not been without trials. This was only one of them. Whether intense financial strain, relational strife, the death of a family member, or infertility issues (among other things), I find myself again and again asking, *Am I really loved, Lord? Will You really come through for me?*

In learning to answer these internal questions in the affirmative, and to really believe He is who He says He is and that He will do what He says He will do, I have encountered many circumstances that called for me to put my growing belief into action. Over the years, I've done this using the practices I explained in the previous chapters. Often the times of silence and solitude, along with the Scripture readings I have chosen, have been the training ground for the day-to-day opportunities to affirm that I am loved, and to believe that "God can do this"—whatever "this" I am being presented with in the moment.

Persevering in Belief for Our Children

Like many other soon-to-be parents who had gone before us, when we found out we were expecting we purchased a book of children's names and began to thumb through it for ideas of what to name this child. After a few months of pondering, we narrowed our list down to three girl names (by this time we knew it was a girl) and knew that one of the three names would become clear as the delivery date approached. Little did I know that God had a different plan.

I was in a seminar one evening when Anna was eight months pregnant, and the presenter was sharing the story of Abraham and Isaac in Genesis 22, in which Abraham was asked by God to sacrifice his son on the alter. What stood out to me that day was that the incident took place on Mt. Moriah. At the end of this story, God provides a ram to sacrifice instead of Abraham having to sacrifice his own son. The speaker finished the telling of the story by quoting Genesis 22:14, "Abraham called the name of that place, *The Lord Will Provide. In the mount of the Lord it will be provided.*"

As that section of teaching came to a close I heard from the Lord, "This is to be your daughter's name." You might imagine the scene at home later that night with my wife. First of all, Moriah wasn't on the short list of three names we were considering. Second, how was I supposed to tell Anna that the Lord had told me our daughter's name? I went home, gave Anna the play-by-play of what had happened that evening, and she responded very graciously. "If that is what the Lord told you, then Moriah it is."

Happily, we now have our own blonde-headed girl running around every day reminding us that "the Lord will provide." I recently wrote this to my daughter Moriah in her tenth birthday card:

MORIAH:

- *Your name means "the Lord will provide" and it's who you are in so many ways! I don't know if we have ever told you, but your mom and I had a hard time getting pregnant. It took over three years and we wondered if we were going to need to adopt. Then one day we found out Mom was pregnant and we were so thrilled!!! The Lord provided you as the first daughter in our family.*

- *Twenty years ago, your Mom and I both left our jobs; she was marketing shoes to fitness instructors and I was working for a business counting money. The Lord called us both to serve Him in full-time ministry. We went to work for Young Life, a ministry to teenagers, and God has provided the money we need to live every day since. Your name is a reminder of how God always takes care of our family.*

- *Your name teaches you and us to put our relationship with God first above everything else. Abraham was willing to sacrifice his only son because he loved God most. God the Father was willing to sacrifice Jesus on the cross because He loved YOU MOST!*

Did you know, Moriah, that you are God's favorite? He is your true Father and He loves you so much. I get to love you too and be your dad here on Earth. I get to provide for you and teach you, but most of all I get to point you to your real Father.

You are loved, Moriah, so, so loved by Him and by me. You are His daughter and you are my daughter and I get to love you alongside with Him. I love it and I love you!

Happy Birthday, Sweet Girl.

Love,
Dad

Moriah was the first of our three children. After our struggle to conceive her, Anna went on to give birth to two more children—our son Elijah and our daughter Hadassah. We have been beyond blessed by God's amazing provision, and His faithfulness in our journey to have a family has strengthened and increased our belief in Him and His love for us.

I always want my children to know how much they are loved, not just by me but by their Heavenly Father. And whether or not it's reflected in their actual name, He is their provider—and mine. That I believe!

Anna's Perseverance

After facing the challenge of infertility, things went well in terms of physical health and wellness in our family for a number of years.

But Anna is very in tune with her body and noticed one day, as I was working on this book, that something wasn't quite right.

She went to see her health practitioner, and after a few months of testing they agreed for her to get a colonoscopy to rule out "worst case scenarios." (She is too young for regularly scheduled colonoscopies so this was a little out of the ordinary.) On the day of her procedure, I went with her to be her driver, since they use light anesthesia during the process. For an hour and a half afterward, I watched the nurse consistently bring out each patient, identify the driver, put the two together, and send them on their way.

Eventually the nurse came out and said, "Shawn Petree." I waited for Anna to walk around the corner so we could head home, but instead the nurse asked me to come with her. As I walked through the door, I knew something wasn't right. Instinctively I began to say, "I believe that you can do this, Lord," over and over again under my breath as the nurse took me to the room where Anna was waiting. She was lying in a bed with her gown still on and the nurse told us the doctor would be in shortly.

Only a few minutes passed until the doctor walked in, sat down next to the bed, and said, "We discovered a tumor in your colon. You have cancer." My now subconscious cadence was on a constant stream, *I believe You can do this, I believe you can do this, Lord*. As you can imagine there were tears and shock, followed by silence. Over the next two weeks, we went to many appointments and Anna underwent a number of scans to determine staging. When it was all said and done, she was diagnosed with Stage III colon cancer.

In the weeks that followed, amidst myriad emotions, we realized that we were faced with the most intense belief journey of our lives, tasked with believing that God could do this, whatever "this" He had for us moving forward. Jesus' words to the hemorrhaging woman became our hope: "Daughter, your *faith* (practical belief)

has made you well; go in peace and be healed of your affliction"
(v.34). But what was our practical belief supposed to look like?
How were we to proceed?

We started with contacting our family and closest friends, asking them to believe on our behalf. We were reminded of the words
of Jesus to the four friends who carried the paralytic on a stretcher
to be healed: "And Jesus, seeing their faith, said to the paralytic,
"Son, your sins are forgiven" (Mark 2:5, NASB). We asked Jesus to
not only consider our faith, but the faith of our friends in Anna's
healing.

When we let our friends know about the situation, one couple
offered to host a prayer gathering at their house on the spur of the
moment. Fifteen of us gathered later that evening, not only to petition to the Lord but also to collectively believe He could do this.
Two days later, Anna I went to a weekly gathering of men that I
am part of, to pray. Thirty men laid hands on us and joined us in
our belief for full and complete healing for Anna. After that, we
widened the circle of friends that we let in on our reality. Soon, we
had people from all over the country, and a few other countries as
well, praying for Anna. People dropped off meals, gift cards, and a
few gathered together to provide a house cleaner for us to take that
responsibility off our plate for the time being. Our community ral-
lied to support us, and we felt very loved and cared for in the midst
of this seemingly impossible situation.

Anna and I, along with our whole family, are very much into
a holistic approach to life, believing that these amazing bodies
the Lord has given us are designed to heal. During Anna's cancer staging it was confirmed she had the slow-growing variety
of cancer. This allowed her to look at many options of treatment,
and she decided on a less invasive version than standard chemo-
therapy and radiation. Five weeks into her diagnosis, Anna spent
a week at a clinic specializing in neurological care. She saw great

improvements from her initial testing when she arrived to her final scan seven days later. She returned home and continued with protocols that she could do at home. In the meantime, we continued to pray and believe that God was doing a great work in her body

One wonderful surprise from God that Anna received during her initial weeks of diagnosis was a vivid dream she had while taking a nap. Anna does not typically remember her dreams, but she was able to remember things from this particular dream in detail.

In the dream, she and I were on a stage at a camp in British Columbia where we have served many times over the years. The room was full of adults and she and I were telling our story of belief. She was specifically telling the crowd how God had healed her and the way her journey with health and belief had drastically increased her faith. As Anna later unpacked this dream with a dear friend of hers, her friend said, "Anna, you have received a promise!"

Her friend went on to remind Anna that the Bible is full of people who receive promises from God. Her friend also pointed out that she has noticed a pattern with God's promises. With each *Promise* there is inevitably a *Problem*, then there is a *Process,* and finally there is *Provision.* We both took this to heart.

Then, a few days after Anna's dream, I came across a scripture that was incredibly encouraging to both Anna and me:

> *Then Jacob departed from Beersheba and went toward Haran. He came to a certain place and spent the night there, because the sun had set; and he took one of the stones of the place and put it under his head, and lay down in that place. He had a dream, and behold, a ladder was set on the earth with its top reaching to heaven; and behold, the angels of God were ascending and descending on it. And behold, the LORD stood above it and said, "I am the LORD, the God of your father Abraham and the God of Isaac; the land on which you lie, I will give it to you and to your descendants. Your descendants will also be like*

the dust of the earth, and you will spread out to the west and to the east and to the north and to the south; and in you and in your descendants shall all the families of the earth be blessed. Behold, I am with you and will keep you wherever you go, and will bring you back to this land; for I will not leave you until I have done what I have promised you." Then Jacob awoke from his sleep and said, "Surely the LORD is in this place, and I did not know it." He was afraid and said, "How awesome is this place! This is none other than the house of God, and this is the gate of heaven." So Jacob rose early in the morning, and took the stone that he had put under his head and set it up as a pillar and poured oil on its top. He called the name of that place Bethel. (Gen. 28:10-19a, NASB)

Not only did we get to read about someone in the Bible having a dream in which he received a promise, but we also got to see God naming a place through a person! This reminded us of the way God named our Moriah, and reminded us how His promise that He will always provide has been such an encouragement to us over the years. In the Genesis story, the name *Bethel* means "house of God." Bethel became a place where God met with His people on a consistent basis—and it all began with a dream and a promise!

Anna and I agree with our friend Cathy that Anna, too, received a promise from God through her dream. Who knows; by the time you are reading this we may have already spoken a number of times at the camp in British Columbia about our journey of belief through Anna's healing! We don't know how it will play out, but we do believe the promise, and we do continue to persevere in belief at this current situation in our lives.

Is there a situation in your life today that seems impossible? Perhaps, like with Anna and me, it's a (seemingly) physical impossibility like infertility or cancer. Or, maybe it's a financial impossibility or a relational one. Whatever it may be, I encourage you to persevere in believing that God is with you, that He is for you, and that "He can do this!"

Anna and I often say to one another, "We are called to do the possible and believe the Lord will do the impossible." I offer you the same hope: we are loved by the God of the impossible!

✦ Belief On-Ramp #10 ✦

For this Belief On-Ramp, there are two questions I want you to consider:

#1. In the "impossible" situation you have identified, what part of the solution (if any) is yours? What is the "possible" you can do right now to partner with God as He is doing His part, the impossible?

#2. In the midst of your impossible situation, have you received a promise from God? If not, perhaps you might consider asking God to give you a promise. Go back to the Genesis 28 story, and read again God's promise to Abraham. You are part of that promise! Look at these two verses again:

> *I am the LORD, the God of your father Abraham and the God of Isaac; the land on which you lie, I will give it to you and to your descendants. Your descendants will also be like the dust of the earth, and you will spread out to the west and to the east and to the north and to the south; and **in you and in your descendants shall all the families of the earth be blessed** (Gen. 28:13-14, NASB, emphasis added).*

God wants to bless you and give you a promise. Ask Him for a specific promise, possibly even a dream. It might come through a reading of Scripture, a line in a worship song you're listening to, an encouragement from a friend, a sermon at church, or any number of sources. God's methods of communication are varied; be listening for the voice of His Spirit as He chooses to reveal Himself.

Maybe you have already heard from God in your impossible situation. If so, what is the Lord's Promise to you? In your situation, can you identify the:

Promise
Problem
Process
Provision

Take some time to identify these and write about them in your journal. This particular Belief On-Ramp may require some time, but I encourage you to stick with it. Persevere in learning to persevere in belief! It will grow your revelation and experience of the fact that YOU ARE LOVED.

Chapter Eleven

Pursuing Deep-Water Friendships

Persevering in belief and living in the assurance that you are loved is no solo gig. In fact, I'll go ahead and say it bluntly: if you are doing life outside of community, you are missing out.

Being able to live out the truest thing God says about you, keeping it in front of you when it becomes opposed, and knowing that you are loved more than you ever imagined, is impossible without friends—and not just friends in the Facebook or Instagram sense of the word. We're talking about deep-water friends. Men and women who see you. The real you.

Friendships like this—"deep-water friendships"—are built through time, intensity of circumstances, and/or because the Father made it happen. Often, all three. Friendships like I've just described have been strong anchors in my life and I would not have been able to believe I am loved without them.

Building a Friendship around Jesus

The deep-water friendship I have with my buddy DCag is one of those strong anchors. That's not his given name, of course, more of a hybrid of his first and last name, pronounced [dee-kag]. We became fast friends in our mid-twenties in between sessions at a

Ken Gire retreat for the Texas and Oklahoma Young Life staff, figuring out the many things we had in common. We'd both recently accepted invitations from each of our mentors to do a two-year internship with the ministry.

The internship began with a training conference at Young Life's Southwind Camp in Central Florida. We were assigned to the same cabin and ended up spending a metric boatload of time together during the three weeks we were there. The training agenda was steeped in worship—it afforded space to get alone with Jesus—and provided heavy portions of learning to care for the emotional and spiritual health of others (and ourselves). Looking back, one might say Southwind was a tone setter for the sort of DNA our friendship would carry into the years ahead. (It was also during those three weeks that DCag and I first met the young lady I got to exchange "I do's" with a couple of years later. Yeah, a story for another time.)

The three weeks in Florida flew by and we returned home, DCag to Tulsa, Oklahoma and me to Big Spring, Texas where we went about our "interning." To say we've "done" a lot together would be an understatement. We've certainly adventured together. We've told our life stories to one another. We've also made it a point to check in with each other on the telephone most weeks, which is a habit we continue to this day, twenty years after that first meeting. I dare say those calls have been some of the holiest moments of my life.

A number of years ago, we read a book together titled *The Supernatural Ways of Royalty*. This book provided a road map for us to further our shared journey of belief. One of the teachings in the book is about the importance of believing that you are great because God created you. For a long season, DCag and I began our weekly call by telling one another that the other is great and making each other repeat this truth out loud on the phone.

This was a powerful part of the process I was going through at the time, which I have been talking about throughout this book: my journey of breaking lies and believing the truth about myself. DCag has been there every step of the way, and I have been able to walk with him in his belief journey as well. Consistency and common experience have melded DCag and me together for the long haul of a life spent following Jesus and learning to believe we are loved.

Jesus Developed Deep Friendships

Jesus modeled the importance of true friendship for us. He had His twelve close companions with whom He did everything for three years. But we learn from the Gospels that three of them—Peter, James, and John—were Jesus' closest friends. We have the most stories about Jesus' friendship with Peter. In fact, there is a story with a similar thread that involves Peter and gives us a picture of friendship and belief. Actually, this story spans over three years. It's sort of a "to be continued" story.

The main character in both stories is Peter. Peter was so devoted to Jesus that he told Him he would die for Him if he had to. When it came down to it, the night Jesus was killed, Peter was asked three times if he knew Jesus. If he said yes, he knew he would likely also be killed. Each of the three times Peter replied, "I don't know that man."

Hold that story in your mind and read this one found in Luke 5: "One day as Jesus was standing by the Lake of Gennesaret, the people were crowding around him and listening to the word of God. He saw at the water's edge two boats, left there by the fishermen, who were washing their nets. He got into one of the boats, the one belonging to Simon, and asked him to put out a little from shore. Then he sat down and taught the people from the boat" (vv. 1-3, NASB).

Scene: Jesus was beginning to gain momentum in His popularity, so much so that people were crowding around Him to listen to His teaching. Being a resourceful guy, Jesus saw a boat that wasn't being used and asked the boat captain if He could borrow the bow of his boat as a makeshift pulpit. Simon (Peter) agreed and put the boat out a little from shore. The story continues:

When He had finished speaking, He said to Simon, "Put out into the deep water and let down your nets for a catch." Simon answered and said, "Master, we worked hard all night and caught nothing, but nevertheless at Your word I will let down the nets." When they had done this, they enclosed a great quantity of fish, and their nets began to break; so they signaled to their partners in the other boat for them to come and help them. And they came and filled both of the boats, so that they began to sink. But when Simon Peter saw that, he fell down at Jesus' feet, saying, "Go away from me Lord, for I am a sinful man!" For amazement had seized him and all his companions because of the catch of fish which they had taken; and so also were James and John, sons of Zebedee, who were partners with Simon. And Jesus said to Simon, "Do not fear, from now on you will be catching men." When they had brought their boats to land, they left everything and followed Him (Luke 5:4-11, NASB).

First off, when we examine this passage, we see that Peter stated the reality, "Master we have toiled all night and caught nothing." Peter looked at the empty nets, looked at the tired fishing crew as they were washing them, and told Jesus the truth about his current situation. He didn't complain and didn't make excuses, but he was honest about the obvious state of affairs. He didn't stop there, however; in fact, Peter followed up that statement with one of the most incredible proclamations of belief in the Gospels:

". . . Nevertheless, at your word I will let down the net." At this stage of the game, Peter didn't even know Jesus personally, but something in him welled up at this newfound friendship.

I have found that belief most often comes on the other side of "nevertheless." It tends to go like this: the reality of a situation is painful, any sort of good outcome looks bleak, and then Jesus shows up just like a good friend. Did you notice that belief and action were required by Peter in order for there to be a different outcome? "I will let down the net." Peter didn't consider the embarrassment or further potential loss of income. Peter just looked at Jesus, loaded up the boys, and headed back out.

Next, notice the invitation of Jesus in verse 4, "Launch out into the deep and let down your nets for a catch." Deep water, the unknown—that is what Jesus invited Peter to consider. That is often what each of us is asked to risk in building deep friendships around Jesus. Once Peter responded with belief and obedience, the provision of fish came in abundance, so much so that it took more than one boat to hold all of the fish—and even at that the boats began to sink.

Peter's response to this miraculous catch of fish was appropriate. He hit his knees in awe and said, "Depart from me for I am a sinful man, O Lord." Peter's little act of belief brought on an overwhelming response by Jesus. And once Peter realized it was the Lord, the fish didn't matter. "When they had brought their boats to land they left everything and followed Him" (v. 11).

For the next three years, the guys who were fishing that day did not leave Jesus' side, especially Peter. Everywhere Jesus went, they were with Him. Peter figured out that life with his friend Jesus was the only life worth living. Being in relationship with God in the flesh was the way to go.

So, we pick up the story three years after this miraculous catch of fish. It was just days after Jesus had been hung on the cross and

His friends were hurting. Peter was especially down because of his denial of Jesus. So Jesus was gone and what did these guys do? They went back to their old life.

> *Afterward Jesus appeared again to his disciples, by the Sea of Galilee. It happened this way: Simon Peter, Thomas (also known as Didymus), Nathanael from Cana in Galilee, the sons of Zebedee, and two other disciples were together. "I'm going out to fish," Simon Peter told them, and they said, "We'll go with you." So they went out and got into the boat, but that night they caught nothing. (John 21:1-3, NASB)*

Scene: Peter and a few of Jesus' friends went back to doing what they did before they met Jesus. Peter likely announced to his friends, "I am going fishing." When the guys decided to join him, I can only imagine what the conversation was like on the boat that night. These guys must have been reminiscing about how amazing it was to have had Jesus with them. My guess is that the conversation also went down the path of what life was like before Jesus. How boring it was, how it lacked meaning. But whatever they might have talked about, as the night came to a close the fellas caught nothing once again. Once again, they had no fish.

We pick it up at, "Early in the morning, Jesus stood on the shore, but the disciples did not realize that it was Jesus. He called out to them, 'Friends, haven't you any fish?' 'No,' they answered. He said, 'Throw your net on the right side of the boat and you will find some.' When they did, they were unable to haul the net in because of the large number of fish" (vv. 4-6, NASB).

"Throw your nets on the right side of the boat." My response to that would have been, *Who does this guy think he is?* But something in their hearts must have remembered that morning three years ago when they came across Jesus and He provided all those fish. So, they threw their nets on the other side of the boat, and immediately they caught so many fish that they couldn't even haul in their nets! The story goes on:

Then the disciple whom Jesus loved said to Peter, "It is the Lord!" As soon as Simon Peter heard him say, "It is the Lord," he wrapped his outer garment around him (for he had taken it off) and jumped into the water. The other disciples followed in the boat, towing the net full of fish, for they were not far from shore, about a hundred yards. When they landed, they saw a fire of burning coals there with fish on it, and some bread(vv. 7-9, NASB).

Peter looked at the fish, and then looked at the man on the shore and said, "It is the Lord." And I just love the next part of this story: Peter realized it was Jesus and immediately jumped into to the water and swam to shore! The nets were full, the old crew was back together, and they were with Jesus.

Jesus said simply, "Come and have some breakfast," and as they ate, none of them dared asked who this man was, for they knew it was the Lord. I think they knew it was Him because of the fish they had caught. They were out all night fishing and caught nothing, and it wasn't the first time this had happened. Then this guy from the shore yells out to try the other side of the boat and they catch a ton of fish! *What these guys were doing previously wasn't working.* They went back to their old life, the one they had before they met Jesus, and that version of life had nothing to offer.

But then Jesus invited them out of the boat and into community with Him and each other. No recrimination. No rebuke. Simply friendship, encouragement, and a fresh calling to believe they were who He'd told them they were all along: His friends. Forever. Friends with a destiny. And it's that same friendship—with Him and with each other—that He invites you and me into, as well.

A "Move a Body" Friend

Brené Brown tells a great story in her book, *Men, Women, and Worthiness,* about getting a call from one of her friends who said, "I just want you to know, Brené, that you are a friend whom I would ask to move a body." Brené thought, *Wow, what does that mean?*

Her friend went on to explain that her other good friend's mom was in town and was an active alcoholic. She (the lady on the other end of the phone call from Brené) received a call that while her friend was away at work her mom had gotten drunk and passed out on the couch. Her friend arrived home and knew that her kids would be returning home from school soon. She had called this friend and asked her to come move her mom off the couch before the kids got home. Shortly thereafter, the two women were moving the passed-out body of the mom from the couch to the guest room.

I chuckled when I read this and had to think, *Hmmmm, whom would I ask to move a body?* Do you have a "move a body" friend? Brené Brown goes on to say in her book that if you have one or two of these types of friends, consider yourself very lucky. If we don't have this type of friend in our life, Brené encourages us to seek out a person with whom we can be vulnerable.

Then, she suggests we all do a few things when life hits us. We contact that person and communicate two main things: *This is what I am feeling. Here is what I need from you.* And if you are on the receiving end of a request from someone who has risked and trusted you with a difficult situation, Brené says the best response is to learn empathy. I love her suggestions for how to do that:

1. **Remove the sting of shame from the situation.** Brené's definition of shame is, "I am bad," which is what people often experience when difficulties arise. (This speaks directly to the theme of lies we have been exploring in this book and the importance

of believing the truth about ourselves. In deep friendships we get to remind one another of the truth and help expel the lies.)

2. **Communicate empathy** through sharing that we have also experienced (and currently experience) shame, not that we understand the specific situation that is being shared by the other person.

3. **Remember, we all know shame!** Empathy is not about connecting to an experience, it is about connecting to an emotion.

Brown concludes by reminding the reader that empathy is often not our default response with our friends. We tend to want to drop off a casserole and run. That is the default. The best response, according to Brené, is, "I don't know what you are going through, but I want to, and I want to be with you in it."

For Anna and me, the day we got the news of Anna's cancer diagnosis was a shock of immense proportion, to say the least. Departing the hospital, as my mind was swirling with a thousand thoughts, one thought was clear: *text Kristi*. Kristi is a "move a body" friend to Anna.

By the time we arrived home, Kristi had picked up our kids from school and was waiting for us at our house. She and Anna hugged and sat and cried together, tried to unpack the shock, and talked about next steps. At one point Kristi said, "Anna, I am with you and Shawn and your family. You know that. I want to know everything as it comes; we are going to walk through this together." I am writing these words five months into Anna's diagnosis and I would say "move a body" friend is a light term for what Kristi and her family have been to Anna and our family.

Having the support of deep-water friend(s) when the challenges of life hit us hard makes all the difference in the world. We all need fellow warriors who are willing to pray, fight. and believe alongside us in the battle as we seek after what Jesus calls "abundant life" (John 10:10). Bottom line: in this journey of seeking out and developing long-term friendships around Jesus, it is incredibly helpful to be vulnerable, build the muscle of empathy, and stay the course together with a few others. Sometimes feeling God's love for us happens through other people who are being the hands and feet of Jesus in our lives. I feel His love for me through them. This has been life changing for me—and I hope it is for you too.

✦ Belief On-Ramp #11 ✦

We can be friends with a number of people on different levels. For example, there are those friendships that develop because you are in close proximity with certain people—like on the job, watching your kids' sports games, neighbors, etc. Many times, when the circumstances change and the proximity is lost, so is the friendship. This is not necessarily bad; it's just a level of friendship. What we're talking about here in this chapter is cultivating deep-water friendships, based on love for God and each other, and on shared values, interests, values, and—over time—experiences.

With that in mind, for this particular Belief On-Ramp, identify your current closest friend(s), the real, long-term kind of friend. Find a way for each of you to listen to Brené Brown's book *Men, Women, and Worthiness* (only available in audio—three hours total of listening). I encourage you to commit to the suggestions she makes in this book as they relate to building depth in your relationship. I also encourage you to explore how you can further develop your friendship around Jesus. If you don't have a closest friend, I encourage you to pray and ask the Lord for that one friend. Commit to being a true friend to another person and allow for the friendship to grow organically.

Whether you're growing a new friendship or developing an older one, the same ideas apply. Do fun things together. (What do you both like to do?) Share meals. Read a Gospel together over the course of a few months. Communicate empathy. Be unwilling to take up offenses. Be vulnerable. And allow for time (this is often hard to do as we want to rush in and create intimacy in months that often takes years to build).

Trust me, the investment is worth it.

Chapter Twelve

Developing Intentional Relationships

There is one other practical aspect of friendship I have deliberately leaned into that has helped me live out this life of faith,
and strengthened me on my journey of coming to believe the truth
that I am loved. It is this: in addition to cultivating several "move
a body" friendships, I have chosen to intentionally "live life" with
a few others. Specifically, I've been meeting with three other men
in a weekly group for 15 years. Actually, that doesn't really describe
what we do. We don't simply meet; we walk through life together.

Early on in this arrangement, my friends and I sensed the
power of a life lived wide open with others. The bond of our
friendships has grown over the years as we continue to access the
incredible power that comes from being intentional and being
together on a consistent basis. Doing life together with these men
has proved to be an integral part of my belief journey. The added
step of writing this book has forced me to articulate the benefits
I've received from being part of these intentional relationships.
I've had to ask myself: What, exactly, is the "do" in "doing life"
together these past 15 years? What does it really look like? How
can I describe it to others? Shortly after asking myself these questions, an example presented itself.

One of the guys shared at our group meeting about something he didn't particularly want to talk about, something he could have easily hidden from us and we would never have known. My friend shared it and said, "It's hard, and I am not proud of the decision I made, but I remain committed to you three brothers. I won't hide. You know it all, the good and the bad." We were able to gather around him and express empathy (as I explained in the last chapter). It was an intimate and transformational moment, not just for him but for all of us. My friend was modeling a way of living life that each of the men in the group has adopted, "Therefore, confess your sins to one another, and pray for one another so that you may be healed." (James 5:16, NASB)

Confession in not all we do in our intentional friendship group, but it is a big part of it. We also share about every aspect of our lives (e.g., walk with God, marriage, being a dad, work, friendships, money, whom we need to reconcile with, how we are giving our time and money away to help others, etc.). In addition, we play. Oh, and we get really mad at one another at times. We say hard things, call each other out on our tendencies, and risk "hurting" one another by stating the truth when we see one of us going "off the rails." Make no mistake: if you choose the hard road of being in an ongoing group with a few it will get messy and take you to the end of yourself—and will hopefully be part of the transformation process of your believing the truth about yourself.

As I think about our group these past 15 years, and other groups I have helped facilitate over the years, I can see how the primary activity of the group has been to reaffirm the truth about each other. To remind one another that we are loved and that we have the ability, through Jesus, to handle anything that comes our way. Oh, and we also just flat out love being together! We do a lot of fun things, go on a couple of overnighters each year together, show up at big events to support one another, and celebrate life together . . . among other things.

Better Together

We used to be a society that centered around family, neighborhoods, and community. It was not unusual for multiple generations to live together under one roof, or, at the very least, in close proximity. People often stayed friends for life with people they knew in grade school.

These days, our culture is much more mobile and individualistic. We tend to be self-sufficient. Fewer and fewer of us live where we were born and raised. Most of our friendships are developed through convenience and proximity, and last as long as the circumstances that brought us together. People attend church much less regularly and tend to move on to another if something bigger and better seems to be going on there. As a society, we can be an individualistic bunch!

But doing life on our own is not part of God's design. He created the world in community (Father, Son, and Holy Spirit) and exists eternally in community. He wants us to experience the love and unity shared by the Godhead, saying at the beginning, "It is not good for the man to be alone . . ." (Genesis 2:18, NLT). We were literally created for community; it's that important to God.

And, it's not only important, it's powerful. Jesus told us in Matthew 18:20 that there is tremendous benefit when two or three of us gather in His name. We can have successes on our own, but God's Word encourages us to gather as friends, and promises there is extra power available to us when we do so. We also read in Hebrews 10:25, ". . . And let us not neglect our meeting together, as some people do, but encourage one another, especially now that the day of his return is drawing near" (NLT).

In good times and bad, God knows how much we need each other and that is one of the reasons He places friends in our lives. Our job is to nurture and cultivate those friendships.

In his book, *Whiter Than Snow: Meditations on Sin and Mercy*, author Paul Tripp says,

> *We weren't created to be independent, autonomous, or self-sufficient. We were made to live in a humble, worshipful, and loving dependency upon God and in a loving and humble interdependency with others. Our lives were designed to be community projects. Yet, the foolishness of sin tells us that we have all that we need within ourselves. So we settle for relationships that never go beneath the casual. We defend ourselves when the people around us point out a weakness or a wrong. We hold our struggles within, not taking advantage of the resources God has given us.*[9]

With this reality in mind, in addition to my group of guys, Anna and I have chosen to walk together with four other couples the past five years with the specific purpose of encouraging one another in our marriages. This, too, has proved to be a vital part of living out of the truth that we are loved by God.

A Group Is Important to Jesus

We see throughout the Gospels that having a group was important to Jesus. In fact, as I mentioned earlier, He spent the majority of His three years of public ministry with Peter, James, and John (His three closest companions), along with the other nine apostles. They ate meals together, traveled, cared for others, took time away, went to parties, and more. Put simply, they lived life together.

Jesus wanted these men with Him through all parts of His public ministry, especially in the significant moments. Jesus' experience of encountering the Father on the mountain was no exception. We read in Matthew 17:1-8,

> *Six days later Jesus took with him Peter and James and John his brother, and led them up on a high mountain by themselves. And he was transfigured before them; and his face shone like the sun, and his garments became as white as light. And behold, Moses and Elijah appeared to them, talking with him. Peter said to Jesus, "Lord, it is good for us to be here; if you wish, I will make three tabernacles here, one for you, and one for Moses, and one for Elijah."* [5] *While he was still speaking, a bright cloud overshadowed them, and behold, a voice out of the cloud said, "This is my beloved Son, with whom I am well-pleased; listen to him!" When the disciples heard this, they fell face down to the ground and were terrified. And Jesus came to them and touched them and said, "Get up, and do not be afraid. And lifting up their eyes, they saw no one except Jesus himself alone." (NASB)*

Two things stand out in the story to me. First, unless we are not privy to other situations in which the Father spoke audibly to Jesus, it had been three years since Jesus heard the voice of His Father out loud. Jesus may have had a sense that something big was going to happen on the mountain that day and He wanted His closest friends there with Him. Sure enough, it was yet another monumental moment and Jesus once again heard those same words the Father had spoken over Him three years earlier: "This is My beloved Son, with whom I am well-pleased; listen to Him!" (v. 5b, NASB)

Now, I'm assuming this got the attention of Peter, James, and John! And that it was alarming, to say the least. No wonder Jesus said to them right out of the gate, "Get up, and do not be afraid" (v. 7b, NASB). In other words, BELIEVE!

As I pointed out earlier, the opposite of fear is belief. Jesus encouraged His friends to *believe*, counting on them to support Him in faith as He was being asked by the Father to believe the truth about Himself. He was asking them to believe that He was the Beloved Son of God, and that He was being called to die—and be raised again to life. We see this in Jesus' next statement: "As they were coming down from the mountain, Jesus commanded them, saying, "Tell the vision to no one until the Son of Man has risen from the dead" (v. 9, NASB).

This little group was being asked to believe, together, that Jesus would rise from the dead and conquer death once and for all. This would not have been an easy thing for any person to believe by himself, even Jesus! Likely recognizing this reality, Jesus invited His three closest companions to be with Him as they headed toward Jerusalem and to the culmination of His destiny. They received the message together, they would process it together, and they would experience it together. Emphasis on the word *together*.

You Can't Go It Alone

I love the passage in Ecclesiastes that says, "Two people are better off than one, for they can help each other succeed. If one person falls, the other can reach out and help. But someone who falls alone is in real trouble. Likewise, two people lying close together can keep each other warm. But how can one be warm alone? A person standing alone can be attacked and defeated, but two can stand back-to-back and conquer. Three are even better, for a triple-braided cord is not easily broken" (Eccl. 4:9-12, NLT). This is God's beautiful plan for relationships.

It was five years ago, as of this writing, that Anna and I chose to intentionally start "doing life" with these four other couples I mentioned. In the midst of the craziness of life and raising young children, we knew enough to know that we all needed support if we were going to keep our marriages a priority.

Our adventure with these other couples began by going on a weekend away together. On this marriage retreat weekend, the speaker, Dr. Tina Schermer Sellers, challenged us to believe that we are loved deeply by God as individuals, and that we are each part of God's mysterious communication of His love by loving one another through the covenant relationship of marriage. We learned the importance of relational intimacy within our marriages, the invitation to deep connection, and the gift of mutual pleasure that God intends for us. We were all deeply impacted—not just as individuals, not just as couples, but as a group—and this experience caused each of us to want to continue to walk together in the message of hope and life for our marriages and families. We knew how much we needed one another.

My friend Doug, who is creeping up on 70 years of age as I write this book, has modeled this kind of intentional friendship for us and many other people. He committed to "doing life together" with some others many years ago, and attributes the richness of his life to this decision. Doug told me how it all began for him: "I was an eager, ambitious young professional dying in a pile. My dad wasn't able to be there for me, wasn't able to say, 'Way to go.' I was desperate for identity. I longed for someone who would take interest in me. A married couple took interest in me. I would go to their house each week for dinner and listen to cassette tapes about God. One particular message stood out from Ephesians 4:16: 'The body builds the body. It builds itself up in love.' From that point on I realized that life is all about relationships with God and people."

Forty years later, Doug is still involved with many of the people he began living life with at that time. In the process, he has learned that the purpose of loving God and receiving God's love in return is not a means to an end. It's an end in itself. The same goes for being *with* people; in God's Kingdom economy, fellowship in Jesus in not a means to an end, it is an end in itself. A mentor once told Doug at age 29: "Invest your life in things that are eternal . . . ," and went on to say, "and I can think of two things that are—to love God and to love people." *

This concept isn't old news. In fact, there is a remarkable research project that has been going on at Harvard for the past 80 years that sheds light on the incredible power of relationships. As reported in the *Harvard Gazette*:

> *When scientists began tracking the health of 268 Harvard sophomores in 1938 during the Great Depression, they hoped the longitudinal study would reveal clues to leading healthy and happy lives. They got more than they wanted. After following the surviving Crimson men for nearly 80 years as part of the Harvard Study of Adult Development, one of the world's longest studies of adult life, researchers have collected a cornucopia of data on their physical and mental health.*
>
> *Of the original Harvard cohort recruited as part of the Grant Study, only 19 are still alive, all in their mid-90s. Among the original recruits were eventual President John F. Kennedy and longtime* Washington Post *editor Ben Bradlee. (Women weren't in the original study because the college was still all male.)*
>
> *In addition, scientists eventually expanded their research to include the men's offspring, who now number 1,300 and are in their fifties and sixties, to find out how early-life experiences affect health and aging over time. Some participants went on to become successful businessmen, doctors, and lawyers, while others ended up as schizophrenics or alcoholics, but not on inevitable tracks.*

---

*Doug Coe to Doug Burleigh at age 29

During the intervening decades, the control groups have expanded. In the 1970s, 456 Boston inner-city residents were enlisted as part of the Glueck Study, and 40 of them are still alive. More than a decade ago, researchers began including wives in the Grant and Glueck studies.

Over the years, researchers have studied the participants' health trajectories and their broader lives, including their triumphs and failures in careers and marriage, and the findings have produced startling lessons, and not only for the researchers.

"The surprising finding is that our relationships and how happy we are in our relationships has a powerful influence on our health," said Robert Waldinger, director of the study, a psychiatrist at Massachusetts General Hospital and a professor of psychiatry at Harvard Medical School. "Taking care of your body is important, but tending to your relationships is a form of self care too. That, I think, is the revelation."

Close relationships, more than money or fame, are what keep people happy throughout their lives, the study revealed. Those ties protect people from life's discontents, help to delay mental and physical decline, and are better predictors of long and happy lives than social class, IQ, or even genes. That finding proved true across the board among both the Harvard men and the inner-city participants.[10]

This Harvard study not only confirms the power of relationship on this journey of life and belief, but it is a reminder that relationships are, in fact, the key to experiencing the life God has for each of us. And that doesn't just mean relationships with others, it's also true of our relationship with our Creator God.

As I have walked this path of belief, learning and growing along the way, I know I could not be where I am without intentionally choosing to walk through life with a few others. I am so grateful for God's leading me in this direction. Anna and I are both experiencing aspects of the abundant life Jesus spoke of in John 10 as we lean deeper and deeper into relationship with God and others.

Sharing This Lifestyle with Others

In my mid-thirties I had tasted enough of the fruit of walking through life with a few intentional friends that I wanted to help others experience what I was experiencing. At the time, I felt like I was hitting on all cylinders in my career. I was eleven years into my career as a director of Young Life. In the community where I was serving at the time, we were seeing a lot of growth—so much so that I found myself in conversations with supervisors about the possibility of taking on a larger territory or possibly training other directors on aspects of the job. At that same time, I was sensing that something was shifting in me around vocation, but was unsure where it would lead.

I knew enough about discernment with regard to big decisions to talk with a mentor and deep-water friend about what was going on in my head. He wisely suggested that we each pray daily for the following thirty days and ask the Lord what He had next in terms of vocation. I still remember where I was sitting early in the morning on Day 23. I had an extended amount of time to sit with God that morning, and I remember saying to Him, "Okay, Father, this is too big of a decision to make on my own. I've been sensing these past few weeks that You are shifting my call from helping teenagers navigate life to helping men do the same thing, but I have no idea what that would look like. Anna and I have two little kids and I can't imagine leaving the security of my current job. So, Father, I am going to sit here until You tell me what to do." And then I sat there and sat there for a while—sitting, waiting.

As you have learned in this book, I have become comfortable with seeking and hearing the voice of God over the years. I believe that He is still speaking, and that He especially appreciates it when we come to Him as a son or daughter asking Him for advice. After sitting for quite a while, I heard these words, not audibly like Jesus did that day on the mountain, but somewhere deep inside of me. The words from God came through so clearly that I was able to write them down in my journal that day: *"Shawn, who's doing this? Who is walking with men through life? Very few. Other people can carry on the work you have been doing with teenagers. I have been training you for this."*

It made sense. My life had been and was being transformed through learning to be with God each day, and through building long-term friendships around Jesus. It seemed natural that I would partner with God in helping many other men similarly experience the abundant life, the "life to the fullest" that Jesus talked about. Jesus' words to His friends after His resurrection resonated with me in a new way: "Go out and train everyone you meet, far and near, in this way of life . . ." (Matt. 28:19, MSG). I felt I was being invited by the Father to do just that with men.

So I did. I put in my resignation two weeks later, leaving a vocation I loved and had giftings for. It was a huge belief step for Anna and me, but this vision of helping others experience what I had been experiencing through growing in Jesus and going deeper into friendship with a few was too clear to ignore. And now, as I have been in this new vocation for almost ten years, I have had the opportunity to walk through life with a lot of men. At the same time, Anna has had been able to walk with women, and our kids (now ages six, 10 and 11) are having the chance to walk closely with their friends in this way too.

Jesus' words are an inspiration and a directive to all of us: to me as an individual, Anna and me as a couple, as well as to the five of us as a family, "(Jesus came) to give his life to set many others free" (Matt. 20:28, Phillips). Isn't that what this life is about? Allowing Jesus to set us free, helping one another to experience more freedom, and, out of our experience of living life to the fullest, helping many other people get free?

I have come to believe that intentional friendship around Jesus with a few intimate relationships is essential to experiencing all God has for us in this life. I hope you will lean in to this idea, and make sure you, too, have a few others close to you. It's available. It's rich. And it's priceless.

✦ Belief On-Ramp #12 ✦

Take an inventory of your life. Who are the few people you are choosing to live life with?

If you already have your "tribe," what are some deliberate ways you can lean in to deep-water friendship with one another more?

If you do not currently have a few people with whom you are intentionally walking through life, ask the Lord whom He would have you invite into your life and then do just that: invite them in. Start a weekly or bi-weekly (or even monthly) group with a few others. Gather multiple couples or families and start to spend time together on a consistent basis, with the intention of knowing, supporting, and encouraging one another. Remember, it will be great and hard and messy and powerful, all at the same time! But it's worth it—so worth it.*

Here is a checklist that may help you as you think and pray about what this might look like for you:

---

*If you would like more direction on building intentional friendships around Jesus visit my friend Ceasar's website at https://www.caesarka-linowski.com/

❏ **Pursue:** Let's face it, most of us enjoy it when other people initiate. But an intentional friendship requires exactly that: intentionality. Whom can you be intentional with? Pick up your phone and call them. Shoot them a quick text or email inviting them to grab a coffee together to catch up. Be the person to make the plans and set it up.

❏ **Listen:** (Don't just talk.) We all love to talk about ourselves. So be the one who gives the other that opportunity. Hear what they're saying and listen to the deeper messages and themes behind what they are saying. This is how we "hear people's hearts" in order to encourage, support, and pray for them. When a friend says that he or she has been feeling lonely lately or been feeling a little depressed, what do you hear? Are you just listening to the fact that they are going through something? Or are you hearing that they need more encouragement or some practical assistance? Be an active listener and really hear what your friends are telling you.

❏ **Be Reliable:** This is true in situations big and small. Be a person of your word. When you make plans with someone, are you frequently changing plans or canceling? When you say you'll be there, will you be there? On time, preferably? Hopefully they'll do the same for you, and your friendship will become something in your life (and theirs) that, in this shifting world, you all know you can count on.

❏ **Be vulnerable:** If we expect to develop and cultivate life-long friendships, we need to be intentional about being vulnerable. We can't expect someone to want to open up to us if we aren't willing to do the same. Be intentional about opening up and asking for prayer or advice. This is really the only way someone will open up to you in return!

❏ **Be empathetic:** As I mentioned in Chapter 11, empathy is not about connecting to an experience, it is about connecting to an emotion. The Bible tells us to "Be happy with those who are happy, and weep with those who weep" (Rom. 12:15, NLT). In a crisis, don't just drop the casserole and run. And don't be too quick to dish out advice. Sometimes we just need to sit with the other in the moment. Intentional friends do this for one another.

❑ **Be an encourager:** This is where we tell each other the truth about them, who God says they are. We remind them they are loved. If a friend is going through a trial, be intentional about speaking and sending words of comfort and encouragement. When they are looking for a job or a house or a car (whatever), root for them, pray for them, send them "good luck" or "I'm praying for you" texts. Be the person who stands with them in every season of life to help push them through and celebrate with them on the other side, and encourages them that God and you are with them!

❑ **Serve:** Everyone has different gifts and abilities; are you using yours to serve your friends? How about your time? The apostle Peter tells us, "God has given each of you a gift from his great variety of spiritual gifts. Use them well to serve one another" (1 Pet. 4:10). Whatever you're gifted at, whatever talent big or small, your friends will feel Jesus' love through you in the practical ways you serve them with the gifts God has given you.

❑ **Pray:** This is one of the most important ways we can cultivate our lifelong, deep-water friendships. But to be intentional about it, we need to know what they need prayer for. Write those prayers down. Maybe start a prayer journal just for your intentional friend group, or make a special section for them in your regular journal. Or, type your requests into the notes section of your phone so you can have it handy all throughout the day. Ask them, from time to time,

"How can I be praying for you?" Then follow up: "Hey, I've been praying for you about such-and-such. How are things going?" This communicates God's love in tremendous ways—and it's so much fun to rejoice together when you see His answers!

Afterword

A few months before Anna and I went on a second marriage retreat with our intentional friend group, each of us in the group received an email from Dr. Tina Sellers, outlining what we were being invited into on the retreat. She wrote,

> *When we feel vulnerable, disconnected, rejected, cranky, it is easy to close our hearts, become unloving—both hard to receive love and not willing to give love. But why? What are our particular triggers that close our hearts? What makes you sensitive? Or stubborn? When do you dig your heels in? What is God trying to teach you in those moments? What would it mean to choose to open your heart anyway? To receive love anyway? To give love anyway?*
>
> *For our weekend away, I am going to ask you to:*
>
> *1. each bring a symbol to represent what moves you away from giving and receiving love. What is it like for you when you are closed? How does it feel? What is your life like? What is your relationship like?*
>
> *2. bring a second symbol. This symbol is to represent how you want to live with a more open heart in your marriage and with your partner—open to giving love and receiving love— even when it is hard. This symbol will represent why you value this openness. What is different for you when your life is open*

like this? What God has for you in an open and loving heart, life, and marriage.

We each showed up to the retreat with our "symbols." Each of us had a chance to present, explain, and walk through our stories in front of one another that weekend. It was powerful!

In addition to this work, Tina invited us to write a letter from God to ourselves. This was the request in Tina's words: "Okay, you have an hour and a half by yourself. Imagine God wants to write a letter to you and He wants you to be the scribe. Go to a place by yourself, pull out your pen and paper, and see what He has to say to you." I received a remarkable word from God that day, my own "transfiguration moment," if you will. I want to share it with you here:

Son,   *10/29/16*

*Can you believe this? Isn't this amazing? You are sitting here on a dock of a lake listening to the sound of water. You are here with your wife (at a marriage retreat) who is not only open to intimacy, connection, and pleasure, but you two are moving toward it together. The theory of being the Beloved that you first heard about 20 years ago, on that Henry Nouwen cassette tape from Chuck, is now your **reality**.*

You believe that you are loved, that you belong. You are part of a family, My family. You know you have a Father who loves you and pursues you. You have a home you actually want to go to each day. You have three remarkable children; you get to be a dad.

I want to remind you of the things you wrote in this journal 10 years ago that you at that time believed at your core:

1. *At some point everyone is going to leave.*
2. *I am a boy and not a man.*
3. *I won't ever be okay (at peace).*

Look at how I have erased those lies and replaced them deeply with the truth these past 10 years, and even more so in these rough past few weeks. Do you see how intimate (and thorough) My love is?

I want to take you back to what we looked at together four years ago in Ephesians 3:16-20, specifically verse 17 in the Greek. It was Paul's ultimate prayer for all who follow Jesus: "That Christ might finally settle down and feel completely at home in your inmost being through your belief in the truth that you are loved."

Son, my Son Jesus has finally settled down and feels completely at home in your inmost being. He does.

*And guess what, son. This picture is no longer who merely you have been **becoming** these past 20 years; this is who you are. **IT'S WHO YOU ARE!***

I trust you with a lot, son. I trust you with Anna. You actually see her and you actually hear her. I trust you with Moriah, Elijah, and Hadassah; are you kidding Me?! Not just anyone gets to be the dad of these kids, my kids.

And I trust you with people, a lot of people. You know it makes no human sense that any one person could manage as many relationships as you do and do it with such integrity, do it well. I was speaking through Dennis a few weeks ago when he said, "You are a keeper of the Father's integrity" (Look up the word "integrity" on your phone.)

Integrity:

1. the state of being complete or whole

2. the condition of being free from damage or defect

I trust you to love people, a lot of people (especially Anna and the kids) with My love. I indwell you in a way that is unique to you. I trust you. Do you hear me, son, really hear me? Look at Me. I trust you.

You believe that you are loved and are free, totally free to give and receive love. Your faith has made you well. You are healed. Go in peace.

- I AM

Needless to say, this letter from God was incredible and so affirming of the reality that I am loved by God. The question I pose with the title of this book, *Am I Loved?*, had been slowly answered over the past twenty years since I had committed to spend daily time with the Father, and this letter from God was the culmination of His answer to that question.

I love God's last line of His letter to me, words Jesus spoke to the woman who washed His feet with her tears and wiped them with her hair just days before He believed the promise of resurrection that He'd spoken of on the mountain with His friends. His words to that woman are also to me: "It is your faith that has saved you. Go in peace" (Luke 7:50, Phillips).

. . . and they are to you as well. Go in peace, my friend, and know you are loved.

About the Author

Out of a long-standing hunger to grow in community and intimacy with God, Shawn Petree has devoted most of his life to learning to hear the Lord's voice, meditate on His word, and discover what God says about His children.

Although his career started in accounting, Shawn felt stirred to something greater. After hearing the whispers of his Father to pursue occupational ministry, Shawn switched gears and has now been serving in various ministry capacities for over 20 years. Although his scope of service has been across the board, it's most prominently been focused on Young Life, and more recently, Teleios—a men's ministry that focuses on growing in Christ through community and friendship with other men.

Shawn holds a Bachelor of Arts degree in Accounting and Finance from Abilene Christian University, and a Master of Divinity degree from Faith Seminary. He lives with his wife Anna and their three children in Seattle, Washington. When he's not serving with Teleios, Shawn enjoys spending time with his family, taking advantage of the beautiful Pacific Northwest outdoors—especially hiking, kayaking, fly fishing—and inviting others into adventure, connection, and rest.

You can reach Shawn at www.amiloved.org.

Endnotes

1. Richo, David, *When Love Meets Fear*, Mahwah, NJ: Paulist Press. 199, p. 112.
2. Charles, Marvin, *Becoming DADS: The Mission to Restore Absent Fathers*, Seattle, WA: Anyman Press, 2016.
3. Job, Reuben P., and Shawchuck, Norman, *A Guide to Prayer for Ministers and Other Servants*. Nashville, TN: Upper Room Books, 1983.
4. Job, Reuben P., and Shawchuck, Norman, *A Guide to Prayer for Ministers and Other Servants*. Nashville, TN: Upper Room Books, 1983.
5. Ephesians 3:18-19 Commentary, Precept Austin, http://www.preceptaustin.org/ephesians_318-19, accessed 5 June 2017.
6. Lewis, C. S., *The Weight of Glory and Other Addresses*. New York: Macmillan, 1949.
7. Thoreau, Henry David, *Walden*, Oxford: Oxford University Press, 1997.
8. Keating, Thomas. *Intimacy With God: An Introduction to Centering Prayer*, New York, NY: The Crossroads Publishing Company, 2015, p. 85.
9. Tripp, Paul David. *Whiter than Snow: Meditations on Sin and Mercy*. Wheaton, IL: Crossway Books, 2008, p. 147.
10. Mineo, Liz, *Harvard Gazette*, "Good Genes are Nice but Joy is Better," April 11, 2017. http://news.harvard.edu/gazette/story/2017/04/over-nearly-80-years-harvard-study-has-been-showing-how-to-live-a-healthy-and-happy-life/. Accessed 1 December, 2017.